What Others Say about Bridge of Faith...

Presented with 'Global Innovation Award' by **Bristol-Myers Squibb**

Nicknamed "The Dynamic Duo" by **Operations Director, a division of Johnson & Johnson**

"...[we had] 453 projects not prioritized or quantified...It's just about identifying what are the vital few projects..."

Andrew Lowe, Operations Director, Ortho-Clinical Diagnostics

"I was able to [get] executive board approval and release of funds for the product development process."

Global Marketing Director, US based multi-national healthcare supply company

"...will teach your people how to fish..."

P.J. Babaoglu, VP WW Process Engineering, a Johnson & Johnson company USA

"Questions to really make you think about your business." Says

Mike Sherwood, Manufacturing Consultant, formerly of Tyco Healthcare

"...this tool will help guide decision making and will improve profitability"

Trevor White, European Business Director, Kodak Clinical Diagnostics

"I anticipate being able to use it in other studies as well"

Sam Narotsky, Management Accountant, a Johnson & Johnson company New York

"Allows you to visualize the 'implications' of decisions and the alternatives" Says

Jenny Abbott, JigSaw Medical Marketing, formerly of Baxter Healthcare

"Identifies the core problem(s) & solution(s)" Says...

Matthew Bergmann Smith, Managing Director, Connector Ltd. (Medical Device & Diagnostics)

More of What Others Say...

"Conventional accounting systems only tell you what you have spent, not how to spend less in the future. Johnson & Johnson will benefit because...cost reduction in the manufacturing organization can eventually benefit everyone, from Shareholders through to Taxpayers... Some projects that had been proposed (through normal 'gut instinct' approach) have been dropped that were not cost-effective, and some new projects have replaced them, with the potential to reduce costs significantly"

David Wild, New Manufacturing Technology Manager,
Johnson & Johnson Clinical Diagnostics

"For many years I have worked on return on investment calculations and used judgement to get the best of out of my spreadsheets and models. The work of reMODEL makes even highly complex and interrelated calculations assessable. The system points you in the 'right direction' and leads you quickly to truly optimal answers that reflect the 'real world'."

Trevor Lewis, Founder & Principal Consultant
Medical Device Consultancy
www.medicaldeviceconsultancy.co.uk

"Bridging the gap between vision and reality" Says...

Kirsten Hemingway-Arnold, Managing Director, Hemingway Corp

Bridge of Faith
For Operations

with examples for
medical device and diagnostic manufacturers

James La Trobe-Bateman
& Lorrie MacGilvray

*"If you don't know where you're going,
any road will take you there."*
George Harrison

© Maravilla Publishing

Bridge of Faith for Operations

With examples for Medical Device and Diagnostic Manufacturers

by James La Trobe-Bateman & Lorrie MacGilvray

Published by:
Maravilla Publishing
http://www.maravillapublishing.com

Cover design by Anthony, Russell & Huw @ www.CC4Web.tv

ISBN 0-9552409-0-5

Acknowledgements and Heartfelt Thank You to…

Mike Lydon for the phrase "Bridge of Faith".

Ian Elliott for the nickname "Dynamic Duo".

David Wild for being a long standing advocate.
PJ Babaoglu for being a long standing advocate.
Mike Sherwood for being a long standing advocate.
John Chemelli for being a long standing advocate.
Fred Marcellus & Leo Kellett for being long standing advocates.
Andrew & Carmel Lowe for being long standing advocates.

Michael Beaumont, David Hulme, Bill Fraser
Matt Gavin, Irene Nichols, Jack Bedard
Charlene McEachen, Frank Yates
Ram Morjaria, Roger Hardacre
Ted Prosser, Wales Innovators Network
Luther & Louise MacGilvray and family
John & Mary La Trobe-Bateman and family
For being long standing advocates and life defining, inspirational mentors.

Eli Goldratt, Kaplan & Cooper, Brian Small, David Frey, Tony Robbins,
Brian Tracy, Mike Litman, Chris Nagy & George Z
For being life defining, motivational inspirations.

PJ Woods for bringing "The Management Team" to life through cartoon.

Huw Owen, Anthony "Ant" McAllister & Russell O'Sullivan at www.cc4web.tv
for helping us finally bring the "Bridge of Faith" to life through their amazing
design & website magic.

Laura Benjamin www.laurabenjamin.com for encouraging, inspiring and
motivating us to write the Bridge of Faith book and series.

reMODEL worldwide clients' excitement, enthusiasm and passion to learn more
about *their Operation* with a broader vision & thinking by using the
"Bridge of Faith"…

James La Trobe-Bateman & Lorrie MacGilvray

This book is dedicated to :

Daughters Ellie & Jenifer for living and breathing the "Bridge of Faith" their entire lives.

Also to those prepared to take the first step onto the Bridge of Faith toward a new, fresh and inspirational way of looking at your entire business and operation.

...Thank you again for taking that leap of faith together with us.

Contents

1. Introduction

What Is a "Bridge of Faith"?

If you are a visionary, you feel that you are already at your destination. It's a great place! In your mind "It's done!" So why do you have difficulty getting others to see it?

If you are not the visionary, you are still a long way from that great place. You have great difficulty seeing what the visionary imagines. Both of you are frustrated by your inability to be there too. There the visionary stands, on the other side of the Grand Canyon, as it were, while everybody else cannot imagine how to ever get there. They fear that it will mean hard work, disruption and absorb resources (and possibly their own money!).

If you are the CEO and know that you must improve, you need a method to bring people with you. If you are at a lower level in the organization, you must prove the value of your suggestions before getting approval to go ahead.

Both types of visionary need to persuade people it is worth crossing that abyss. They need to construct a "bridge" to minimize the Leap of Faith that people are being asked to make.

That's the metaphor.

Real Questions about Your Business

You have probably got concrete questions, such as:

- How do I justify proposals for change?
- How do we become more profitable with the least effort?
- How do I convince myself that my idea is great?
- How do we go about designing a new product for manufacturability?
- Which process should be improved?
- Where are the key levers to the biggest improvement?
- How does this change affect the whole operation?
- Where should we deploy our improvement people?

This book is about the nuts and bolts of answering these questions.

It describes a method to bridge the gulf between shop floor terms and business measures. It uses numbers to help everybody understand. Crossing this bridge before making any commitment provides the confidence and conviction to do it.

The methodology has been developed by **reMODEL Consultants International Ltd** over 15 years. They have proven its value in the course of their business with large and small suppliers to the healthcare industry.

The fundamental concept is applicable to all business functions. Indeed, it takes all parts of the organization to co-operate to reap the benefits of any improvement. Operations, finance, marketing, sales, product design and development from the shop floor to the CEO need to be able to see the same picture.

How Does It Work?

The book introduces concepts one at a time and gradually increases in complexity with each scenario. The learning comes from having to think through every issue. You can check your answers and find more explanation at the book's website **www.BridgeOFaith.com**

If you like logical puzzles, then this is *really* for you.

Visualizing the Problem

Business managers pay attention to information that tells them how well the business is doing.

The shop floor is preoccupied with a range of different facts and figures, including machine speeds, waste, manning levels, batch sizing policy, stock policy, shift patterns.

Improvement calls for change on the shop floor. But how does shop floor information relate to business measures?

How can the shop floor instigate change without understanding its implications?

How can the business managers agree to change without seeing the effect on their measures?

Neither party talks the language of the other. Nonetheless they must communicate.

At the top is the business manager's view.

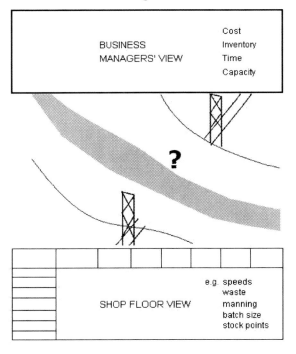

At the bottom is a more complex set of shop floor data

How the Scenarios Are Laid Out

Each scenario is displayed on opposing pages.

At the top are the business measures. On the left are the actual output figures. On the right are the differences created by the change.

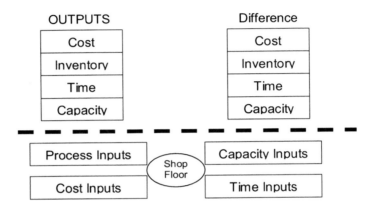

Below the dotted line, the shop floor view is divided into 4 groupings: related to Process Description, Variable Cost inputs, Capacity inputs and Time and Inventory inputs.

Further detail is provided by listing the inputs for each process step. Everything interacts to create the business performance summarized at the top of each page. The minimum data needed is used to provide the most management information.

In order to make the learning easier, we are going to introduce the key management measures one at a time, until they are all in use. Then we will look at the interactions between all of them.

We will look first at Cost.

2. COST

Cost Outputs

Cost is broken down into Activity Based Costing groups as follows:

- **VOLUME** related expense varies in proportion to the *volume shipped*

It includes:
Materials
Some Production labor
Wear and tear maintenance
Some Quality Control

- **BATCH** related expense varies in proportion to the *number of batches*

It includes:
Some Production labor
Some Quality Control
Some Customer support
Manufacturing support
Some Materials management

- **PRODUCT** related expense varies in proportion to the *number of products*

It includes:
Some Quality Assurance
Some Customer support
Product technical support
Regulatory affairs
Product dossier control
Some Materials management

- **FACILITY** related expense remains if nothing is made

It includes:
General management and admin
Some Quality Assurance
Routine maintenance
Facilities Engineering support
Rent, rates & utilities

Process Inputs

This is what the shop floor terms mean:

Activity
: A process that involves use of Material, Labor or Time resource.

Qty per Sale
: The amount of this component that is built into the finished item for sale. E.g. If the unit of sale is a "kit" and there are 10 bottles in it, then "10" is the figure entered here.

Unit
: The unit of measure for the component in this activity.

Run Waste
: The amount of waste which varies in proportion to volume.

    Examples are QC rejects and process yield.

Fixed Batch Waste
: The fixed amount wasted every time a batch of this component is made. Examples are pump priming, calibration samples, fluid left in pipes or tanks. The amount is the same regardless of batch size.

Batch Size Information is entered one of these 3 ways:

Batch Size
: The fixed batch size, if fixed.

Batches per Year
: The number of batches per year, if made at fixed intervals. Batch size varies with demand.

Same Good Batches per Year as other task?
: If this activity is done whenever another is done, this figure is the task reference number of that activity.

Variable Cost Inputs

Items per minute
The average throughput rate whilst the line is running (i.e. not being set up). Includes all normal running hiccups and short stoppages. It is lower than the rated line speed.

Batch Changeover Time
The sum of all the things that happen between batches i.e. setup, clean, line clearance. Measure from the ***"last good one out of batch 1 to first good one out of batch 2".***

Manning (Each Line)
The number of employees present during Run and Changeover

Non Value Adding Hours per Hour
This allows for all the time that production staff are in discussions, doing paperwork, having breaks, vacations & sickness, being trained, etc. Also includes other productive activities not included in the operational data for that activity.

Usually in the range 0.5 – 2

Labor Rate per Hour
Annual salary divided by 52 x Hours per Week worked. The effect of holidays, etc is covered by NVA hours per hour.

Employer Costs per Hour
Effective average hourly cost of employer benefits including insurance, pension, subsidized site services

Material Value Added
The purchase cost of the materials or bought in services used in this activity. Cost per item.

Cost Scenarios

#01 Simple Factory: Cost

Let's look first just at the Cost for an operation described as a single process.

In this exercise, as in all the others, a change has been made and you will have to work out what the change was.

The management information is at the top. On the left are the predicted values after the change is made. On the opposite page are the differences caused by the change.

Underneath are the two tables that contain the shop floor data that describe the process and variable cost inputs.

Predicted Values after Change   250,000 items/yr

COST	Material	Other	per item
VOLUME	$334,225	$317,513	$2.607
BATCH		$7,620	$0.030
PRODUCT		$0	$0.000
FACILITY		$280,000	$1.120
TOTAL	**$939,358**		**$3.76**

Process Description before Change

Task ref	Activity	Qty per sale	unit	Run waste	Fixed Batch waste	Batch size	Batches per Year	Same Batches per Year as other task?
1	All-in-one process	1	pack	15%	300	2,500		

Variable Cost Inputs before Change

Task ref	Activity	Items per Minute	Batch Change over Hours	Manning	Non Value Adding Hours per Hour	Labor Rate per Hour	Employer Costs per Hour	Material Value Added
1	All-in-one process	2	0.5	3	1.0	$15.00	$4.00	$1.25

Question:
Which input in the Variable Cost table, if changed by 20%, would cause the change shown in the difference table below?

Answer:
This is worked through below.

Differences

Cost Change	Material	Other	per item
VOLUME	-$83,556	$0	-$0.334
BATCH		$0	$0.000
PRODUCT		$0	$0.000
FACILITY		$0	$0.000
TOTAL	-$83,556		-$0.334

Calculation

Material cost before change = 334225+83556 = 417581

Thus cost saving = 83556/417581 = 20%

This would happen if the material purchase price was reduced by 20% from $1.25 to $1.00

#02 Simple Factory: Cost

This is the same operation as the last exercise.

We will continue to explore the effect of different shop floor changes.

This time try to work it out for yourself.

Predicted Values after Change 250,000 items/yr

COST	Material	Other	per item
VOLUME	$417,781	$158,757	$2.306
BATCH		$7,620	$0.030
PRODUCT		$0	$0.000
FACILITY		$280,000	$1.120
TOTAL		**$864,158**	**$3.46**

Process Description

Task ref	Activity	Qty per sale	unit	Run waste	Fixed Batch waste	Batch size	Batches per Year	Same Batches per Year as other task?
1	All-in-one process	1	pack	15%	300	2,500		

Variable Cost Inputs

Task ref	Activity	Items per Minute	Batch Change over Hours	Manning	Non Value Adding Hours per Hour	Labor Rate per Hour	Employer Costs per Hour	Material Value Added
1	All-in-one process	2	0.50	3	1.0	$15.00	$4.00	$1.25

Question:
Which input in the Variable Cost table would cause the change shown in the difference table below?

How much has it changed?

Hint:
Look in the detail of the Cost change table. All of the difference is in volume related non-material cost. This time you are looking for something related to labor. Note also that batch related cost does not change.

Answer:
Can be found at www.BridgeoFaith.com

Differences

Cost Change	Material	Other	per item
VOLUME	$0	-$158,757	-$0.635
BATCH		$0	$0.000
PRODUCT		$0	$0.000
FACILITY		$0	$0.000
TOTAL		-$158,757	-$0.635

#03 Simple Factory: Cost

We continue with the single process operation of the last two exercises.

Try another simple change.

Predicted Values

250,000 items/yr

COST		Material	Other	per item
	VOLUME	$417,781	$317,513	$2.941
	BATCH		$4,572	$0.018
	PRODUCT		$0	$0.000
	FACILITY		$280,000	$1.120
	TOTAL	**$1,019,866**		**$4.08**

Process Description

Task ref	Activity	Qty per sale	unit	Run waste	Fixed Batch waste	Batch size	Batches per Year	Same Batches per Year as other task?
1	All-in-one process	1	pack	15%	300	2,500		

Variable Cost Inputs

Task ref	Activity	Items per Minute	Batch Change over Hours	Manning	Non Value Adding Hours per Hour	Labor Rate per Hour	Employer Costs per Hour	Material Value Added
1	All-in-one process	2	0.5	3	1.0	$15.00	$4.00	$1.25

Question:

Which input in the Variable Cost table would cause the change shown in the difference table below?

How much has it changed?

Hint:

A look at the difference table shows that the change is purely batch related with no affect on material cost.

Answer at www.BridgeoFaith.com

Differences

Cost Change	Material	Other	per item
VOLUME	$0	$0	$0.000
BATCH		-$3,048	-$0.012
PRODUCT		$0	$0.000
FACILITY		$0	$0.000
TOTAL		-$3,048	-$0.012

#04 Simple Factory: Cost

This is still the same operation as the previous exercises.

The relationships are now a bit more complex.

Predicted Values

250,000 items/yr

COST	Material	Other	per item
VOLUME	$417,781	$211,676	$2.518
BATCH		$5,080	$0.020
PRODUCT		$0	$0.000
FACILITY		$280,000	$1.120
TOTAL		$914,537	$3.66

Process Description

Task ref	Activity	Qty per sale	unit	Run waste	Fixed Batch waste	Batch size	Batches per Year	Same Batches per Year as other task?
1	All-in-one process	1	pack	15%	300	2,500		

Variable Cost Inputs

Task ref	Activity	Items per Minute	Batch Change over Hours	Manning	Non Value Adding Hours per Hour	Labor Rate per Hour	Employer Costs per Hour	Material Value Added
1	All-in-one process	2	0.50	3	1.0	$15.00	$4.00	$1.25

Question:
Which input in the Variable Cost table would cause the changes shown in the difference table below?

How much has it changed?

There are 2 possible answers.

Hint:
The difference table has 2 changes. It looks like a labor issue, and you need to work out whether there is a batch size issue or not.

Answer at www.BridgeoFaith.com

Differences

Cost Change	Material	Other	per item
VOLUME	$0	-$105,838	-$0.423
BATCH		-$2,540	-$0.010
PRODUCT		$0	$0.000
FACILITY		$0	$0.000
TOTAL		-$108,378	-$0.434

#05 Simple Factory: Cost

This is still the same operation as the previous examples.

We are now looking at effects over a broader front than the previous examples.

In this case, one change affects material, volume related labour and batch related labour.

Predicted Values

250,000 items/yr

COST	Material	Other	per item
VOLUME	$382,966	$291,054	$2.696
BATCH		$6,985	$0.028
PRODUCT		$0	$0.000
FACILITY		$280,000	$1.120
TOTAL		$961,005	$3.84

Process Description

Task ref	Activity	Qty per sale	unit	Run waste	Fixed Batch waste	Batch size	Batches per Year	Same Batches per Year as other task?
1	All-in-one process	1	pack	15%	300	2,500		

Variable Cost Inputs

Task ref	Activity	Items per Minute	Batch Change over Hours	Manning	Non Value Adding Hours per Hour	Labor Rate per Hour	Employer Costs per Hour	Material Value Added
1	All-in-one process	2	0.50	3	1.0	$15.00	$4.00	$1.25

Question:
Which input in the Process Description table would cause the changes shown in the difference table below?

How much has it changed?

Hint:
There are 2 possible Process changes, but neither is in production planning.

Answer at www.BridgeoFaith.com

Differences

Cost Change	Material	Other	per item
VOLUME	-$34,815	-$26,459	-$0.245
BATCH		-$635	-$0.003
PRODUCT		$0	$0.000
FACILITY		$0	$0.000
TOTAL		-$61,910	-$0.248

#06 Simple Factory: Cost

This is the same operation as the previous exercises.

This exercise is to remind ourselves that not all cost savings come from examining process flows!

Predicted Values

250,000 items/yr

COST		Material	Other	per item
	VOLUME	$417,781	$317,513	$2.941
	BATCH		$7,620	$0.030
	PRODUCT		$0	$0.000
	FACILITY		$255,000	$1.020
	TOTAL	**$997,914**		**$3.99**

Process Description

Task ref	Activity	Qty per sale	unit	Run waste	Fixed Batch waste	Batch size	Batch per Year	Same Batches per Year as other task?
1	All-in-one process	1	pack	15%	300	2,500		

Variable Cost Inputs

Task ref	Activity	Items per Minute	Batch Change over Hours	Manning	Non Value Adding Hours per Hour	Labor Rate per Hour	Employer Costs per Hour	Material Value Added
1	All-in-one process	2	0.50	3	1.0	$15.00	$4.00	$1.25

Question:

None of the Process or Variable Cost inputs has changed here.

What else might have caused the change?

Answer at www.BridgeoFaith.com

Differences

Cost Change	Material	Other	per item
VOLUME	$0	$0	$0.000
BATCH		$0	$0.000
PRODUCT		$0	$0.000
FACILITY		-$25,000	-$0.100
TOTAL		-$25,000	-$0.100

3. INVENTORY

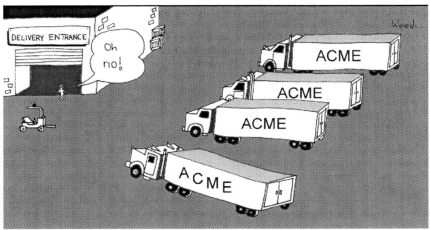

Why Is Inventory Important?

Take a small business view. If you are running a shop, you have to buy stock before you can sell it. You usually have to pay for it before you get the money back from your customers. This means that you have to find the cash to finance the purchase. The stock represents a financial investment on which you hope to make a return by selling things. It is a risk. It means tying up cash that could be used for other, more productive things.

Finance View of inventory

Management accountants value inventory as "fully burdened". This means that it does not simply include the material value, but also the labor it takes to process that material and an allocation of other operating expense that has nothing to do with processing material. So they take one number and factor it, sometimes by quite a large number.

Shop Floor View of Inventory

The shop floor sees inventory as piles of material lying around. Measuring it as material value closely fits with this view. If the pile is twice as big, then it is "worth" twice as much.

Which View Is Best?

Because we need to take both the management view and the shop floor view, we will report the figure both ways. Occasionally the two contradict: what looks good to finance looks crazy to the shop floor and vice versa. Some of the Scenarios illustrate this. To arbitrate we suggest going back to the reason why inventory is important. Does the change mean tying up more cash?

Inventory Cost

Talking about inventory as a "cost" often leads to confusion. However, in some companies, inventory is assigned a cost to acknowledge that having it causes expense, e.g. running a warehouse. Divisions of large companies may even be charged a percentage of their inventory value in order to encourage them to minimize inventory. In this book, we will not use it, and will pay attention to inventory in other ways. If there are warehousing costs, then these are considered operating expenses.

Types of Inventory

In the scenarios that follow, inventory is split into different categories:

Raw Material

- Material received into the operation and stored ready for processing.
- It is assumed to be received in relatively large quantities and gradually depleted by use before the next delivery. If you watched the inventory level with time you would see it varying in a saw tooth pattern:

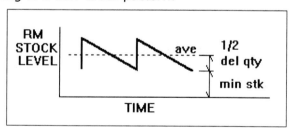

The sharp rises correspond to deliveries and the slope its gradual use.

In Process part of WIP

- This is material which has "left" one stocking point and has not yet "arrived" at another.
- It is what is being worked on at any moment in time
- For products with a shelf life, you can think of it as the amount of material that would be scrapped if everybody suddenly deserted their posts and did not come back for a long time

Intermediate Stock part of WIP

- This is material which has been processed to a part finished state and is held in intermediate storage.
- When the Input table contains a non-zero number, it is assumed that stock is held in a saw tooth manner (as for Raw Material).
- The value is the sum of all the materials that were used to make it.

Finished Goods

- This is material finished and held in stock awaiting sale.
- When the Input table contains a non-zero number, it is assumed that stock is held in a saw tooth manner. It jumps up just after a new batch has been completed and then gradually drops as orders are fulfilled.
- Its value is the sum of all the materials that were used to make the product.

Inventory and Time Inputs

This is what the shop floor terms mean.

Varieties	The number of variants of this component. Examples are Products, Packaging Types or Sizes.
RM Min Days Stock	The number of days supply of Raw Material to be held as safety stock
RM Days between Deliveries	How often the supplier delivers raw material. Usually negotiated between purchasing and the supplier
Intermediate Days Hold Time	The number of calendar days that a *complete* batch is held before being able to pass to store or to the next process step. Examples are maturing processes or quality assurance review time. Set by product and process designers.
Intermediate Days Min Saw tooth)	If the item is stocked at this point (rather than just held waiting for the next process), enter the minimum stock level in days supply. A saw tooth pattern is assumed unless this is 0. This is usually determined by production planning.
Finished Goods Days Hold Time	The number of calendar days that a *complete* batch is held before being sold. In a regulated industry it is often common to delay approval for sale after completion awaiting a 3rd party approval or microbiology test
Finished Goods Days Min Stock	If the item is stocked at this point (rather than just held waiting for the next process), the minimum stock level in days supply. This is typically the distributor's safety stock level, set to cover uncertainty of demand.

This set of inputs more directly relate to timing through the operation. However, the next few Scenarios will look at inventory effects only.

Inventory Scenarios

#07 Simple Factory: Inventory

The previous 6 examples looked only at Cost. Now, we are going to introduce Inventory.

There is an additional Output table for inventory and an output difference table on the opposite page. Note that the ML&O (fully burdened value) is rounded.

There is also an additional Inventory Input table at the bottom of the opposite page.

The first exercise involves a change that only affects inventory, leaving cost unaltered.

Predicted Values

250,000 items/yr

COST	Material	Other	per item
VOLUME	$417,781	$317,513	$2.941
BATCH		$7,620	$0.030
PRODUCT		$0	$0.000
FACILITY		$280,000	$1.120
TOTAL	**$1,022,914**		**$4.09**

INVENTORY	Material only	ML&O
Raw Material	$13,735	$13,700
WIP	$4,273	$10,500
Finished	$9,575	$23,400
All	**$27,583**	**$47,600**

Process Description

Task ref	Activity	Qty per sale	unit	Run waste	Fixed Batch waste	Batch size	Batches per Year	Same Batches per Year as other task?
1	All-in-one process	1	pack	15%	300	2,500		

Variable Cost Inputs

Task ref	Activity	Items per Minute	Batch Change over Hours	Manning	Non Value Adding Hours per Hour	Labor Rate per Hour	Employer Costs per Hour	Material Value Added
1	All-in-one process	2	0.5	3	1.0	$15.00	$4.00	$1.25

Question:
Which of the Inventory inputs would cause the changes shown in the difference table?

Hints:
Look first at the output difference tables. The only change is to Raw Material inventory.

In theory there are 2 possible answers, but in practice only one is realistic.

Answer is at www.BridgeoFaith.com

Differences

Cost Change	Material	Other	per item
VOLUME	$0	$0	$0.000
BATCH		$0	$0.000
PRODUCT		$0	$0.000
FACILITY		$0	$0.000
TOTAL		$0	$0.000

Inventory Change	Material only	ML&O
Raw Material	-$10,301	-$10,300
WIP	$0	$0
Finished	$0	$0
All	-$10,301	-$10,300

Inventory Inputs

Task ref	Varieties	RM Min Days Stock	RM Days between Deliveries	Intermed Days Hold Time	Intermed Days Min Sawtooth	Finished Goods Days Hold Time	Finished Goods Days Min Stock
1	1	14	14				7

#08 Simple Factory: Inventory

This is still the same operation of the previous exercises.

This exercise further explores inventory.

Predicted Values

250,000 items/yr

COST	Material	Other	per item
VOLUME	$417,781	$317,513	$2.941
BATCH		$7,620	$0.030
PRODUCT		$0	$0.000
FACILITY		$280,000	$1.120
TOTAL		**$1,022,914**	**$4.09**

INVENTORY	Material only	ML&O
Raw Material	$24,037	$24,000
WIP	$4,273	$10,500
Finished	$2,707	$6,600
All	**$31,017**	**$41,100**

Process Description

Task ref	Activity	Qty per sale	unit	Run waste	Fixed Batch waste	Batch size	Batches per Year	Same Batches per Year as other task?
1	All-in-one process	1	pack	15%	300	2,500		

Variable Cost Inputs

Task ref	Activity	Items per Minute	Batch Change over Hours	Manning	Non Value Adding Hours per Hour	Labor Rate per Hour	Employer Costs per Hour	Material Value Added
1	All-in-one process	2	0.5	3	1.0	$15.00	$4.00	$1.25

Question:

Which of the Inventory inputs would cause the changes shown in the difference table?

Hint:

The change is just to Finished Goods.

Answer at www.Bridgeo Faith.com

Differences

Cost Change	Material	Other	per item
VOLUME	$0	$0	$0.000
BATCH		$0	$0.000
PRODUCT		$0	$0.000
FACILITY		$0	$0.000
TOTAL		$0	$0.000

Inventory Change	Material only	ML&O
Raw Material	$0	$0
WIP	$0	$0
Finished	-$6,868	-$16,800
All	-$6,868	-$16,800

Inventory Inputs

Task ref	Varieties	RM Min Days Stock	RM Days between Deliveries	Intermed Days Hold Time	Intermed Days Min Sawtooth	Finished Goods Days Hold Time	Finished Goods Days Min Stock
1	1	14	14				7

#09 Simple Factory: Cost & Inventory

This is example #01 with inventory added.

We previously looked at the cost impact.

We are now looking at the inventory impact of the same change.
The effect is on all types of inventory.

Predicted Values

250,000 items/yr

COST	Material	Other	per item
VOLUME	$334,225	$317,513	$2.607
BATCH		$7,620	$0.030
PRODUCT		$0	$0.000
FACILITY		$280,000	$1.120
TOTAL		**$939,358**	**$3.76**

INVENTORY	Material only	ML&O
Raw Material	$19,229	$19,200
WIP	$3,419	$9,600
Finished	$7,660	$21,500
All	**$30,308**	**$50,300**

Process Description

Task ref	Activity	Qty per sale	unit	Run waste	Fixed Batch waste	Batch size	Batch per Year	Same Batches per Year as other task?
1	All-in-one process	1	pack	15%	300	2,500		

Variable Cost Inputs

Task ref	Activity	Items per Minute	Batch Change over Hours	Manning	Non Value Adding Hours per Hour	Labor Rate per Hour	Employer Costs per Hour	Material Value Added
1	All-in-one process	2	0.5	3	1.0	$15.00	$4.00	$1.25

Question:

Can you rationalise why a change to one input in the
Variable Cost table would cause all the changes shown in
the difference table?

Hint:

Look back at exercise #01

Answer at www.BridgeoFaith.com

Differences

Cost Change	Material	Other	per item
VOLUME	-$83,556	$0	-$0.334
BATCH		$0	$0.000
PRODUCT		$0	$0.000
FACILITY		$0	$0.000
TOTAL	-$83,556		-$0.334

Inventory Change	Material only	ML&O
Raw Material	-$4,807	-$4,800
WIP	-$855	-$900
Finished	-$1,915	-$1,900
All	-$7,577	-$7,600

Inventory Inputs

Task ref	Varieties	RM Min Days Stock	RM Days between Deliveries	Intermed Days Hold Time	Intermed Days Min Sawtooth	Finished Goods Days Hold Time	Finished Goods Days Min Stock
1	1	14	14				7

#09

#10 Simple Factory: Cost & Inventory

This is the same operation as before.

This exercise involves changes to cost and inventory.

Here we look at the difference between fully burdened inventory and material inventory.

Predicted Values

250,000 items/yr

COST	Material	Other	per item
VOLUME	$417,781	$238,135	$2.624
BATCH		$5,715	$0.023
PRODUCT		$0	$0.000
FACILITY		$280,000	$1.120
TOTAL		**$941,631**	**$3.77**

INVENTORY	Material only	ML&O
Raw Material	$24,037	$24,000
WIP	$4,273	$9,600
Finished	$9,575	$21,600
All	**$37,885**	**$55,200**

Process Description

Task ref	Activity	Qty per sale	unit	Run waste	Fixed Batch waste	Batch size	Batches per Year	Same Batches per Year as other task?
1	All-in-one process	1	pack	15%	300	2,500		

Variable Cost Inputs

Task ref	Activity	Items per Minute	Batch Change over Hours	Manning	Non Value Adding Hours per Hour	Labor Rate per Hour	Employer Costs per Hour	Material Value Added
1	All-in-one process	2	0.5	3	1.0	$15.00	$4.00	$1.25

10

Question:
Which input in the either of Process, Variable Cost or Inventory input tables causes the strange Inventory changes?

Hint:
This cannot be a material change, because neither material cost nor material inventory change. Neither can it be a timing change, because the material inventory is unaffected.

Answer at www.BridgeoFaith.com

Differences

Cost Change	Material	Other	per item
VOLUME	$0	-$79,378	-$0.318
BATCH		-$1,905	-$0.008
PRODUCT		$0	$0.000
FACILITY		$0	$0.000
TOTAL		-$81,283	-$0.325

Inventory Change	Material only	ML&O
Raw Material	$0	$0
WIP	$0	-$900
Finished	$0	-$1,800
All	$0	-$2,700

Inventory Inputs

Task ref	Varieties	RM Min Days Stock	RM Days between Deliveries	Intermed Days Hold Time	Intermed Days Min Sawtooth	Finished Goods Days Hold Time	Finished Goods Days Min Stock
1	1	14	14				7

#11 Simple Factory: Cost & Inventory

This is still the same operation.

We now look at a single Process change that reduces material cost, labour cost, and raw material inventory, while increasing Work In Progress and finished goods.

This type of change has far-reaching impacts.

It is a key lever for operations management.

Predicted Values   250,000 items/yr

COST	Material	Other	per item
VOLUME	$391,114	$297,247	$2.753
BATCH		$3,567	$0.014
PRODUCT		$0	$0.000
FACILITY		$280,000	$1.120
TOTAL		**$971,927**	**$3.89**

INVENTORY	Material only	ML&O
Raw Material	$22,502	$22,500
WIP	$7,907	$19,600
Finished	$10,626	$26,400
All	**$41,035**	**$68,500**

Process Description

Task ref	Activity	Qty per sale	unit	Run waste	Fixed Batch waste	Batch size	Batches per Year	Same Batches per Year as other task?
1	All-in-one process	1	pack	15%	300	2,500		

Variable Cost Inputs

Task ref	Activity	Items per Minute	Batch Change over Hours	Manning	Non Value Adding Hours per Hour	Labor Rate per Hour	Employer Costs per Hour	Material Value Added
1	All-in-one process	2	0.5	3	1.0	$15.00	$4.00	$1.25

11

Questions:

What Process change caused this effect?

Why does some inventory increase and some decrease?

Hint:

Look first for the cause of the batch related cost change

Answer at www.BridgeoFaith.com

Differences

Cost Change	Material	Other	per item
VOLUME	-$26,667	-$20,267	-$0.188
BATCH		-$4,053	-$0.016
PRODUCT		$0	$0.000
FACILITY		$0	$0.000
TOTAL		-$50,987	-$0.204

Inventory Change	Material only	ML&O
Raw Material	-$1,534	-$1,500
WIP	$3,634	$9,100
Finished	$1,051	$3,000
All	$3,151	$10,600

Inventory Inputs

Task ref	Varieties	RM Min Days Stock	RM Days between Deliveries	Intermed Days Hold Time	Intermed Days Min Sawtooth	Finished Goods Days Hold Time	Finished Goods Days Min Stock
1	1	14	14				7

Leading Edge organizations depend on their ability to adapt rapidly to changed environments, as…

"The rate of change is not going to slow down anytime soon. If anything, competition in most industries will probably speed up even more in the next few decades."

John P. Kotter, Leadership Now

4. RESPONSE & LEAD TIME

Introducing "Response Time"

Response time is defined here in a way that is probably new to most people.

When people talk about "responsiveness", they can mean one of 2 different things. It can mean "how nimble is the management?" Is it very quick to react to change? Does it solve crises very quickly? This responsiveness relates to a quality of management.

Another kind of responsiveness is intrinsic to the nature of the operation. Compare the intrinsic ability of a supertanker to change course with that of a jet-ski. However good the crew, the tanker cannot change course faster than a jet-ski.

We shall use the second meaning of the term

Why Measure Response Time?

Response time is important is because it is a measure of the ease with which manufacturing can change its output to meet changes in demand.

A more responsive operation:

- Is less likely to default on customer orders
- Has fewer disruptive changes to production plans
- Is in less of a panic

What about Lead Time?

We make a distinction between Response Time and the more commonly used phrase "Lead Time". This is the time elapsed from when a material is drawn from stock until the batch is ready for shipment. It includes any time when it may be "held" awaiting maturation, QA clearance or some other known delay. Lead Time contributes to Response Time.

In simple terms, Lead Time is the time it takes to make something.

How is Response Time Defined?

Response Time is the longest time it takes to fulfill an unforecast large order without changing production schedules.

RESPONSE TIME = Batch Interval + Lead Time

You can remember this formula by analogy. If you were planning to travel from A to B by train, how much time should you allow to be sure of getting there? We take the worst case, which is when you have just missed one. You then have to wait for the next plus wait for the time it takes to arrive at the destination.

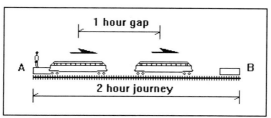

i.e.: Allowed Time = Interval between trains + Journey Time which equals 1 + 2 = 3 hours in this example.

It is possible to talk about the response time for intermediate components too. However, it only makes sense if the intermediate is stocked. ("Trains must stop at the station")

What Things Reduce Response Time?

- Making batches more frequently i.e. reducing batch size

- Reducing lead time

- Introducing stocking points

Reducing response time to the end customer is one reason why you might use a finished goods distributor. You might also have to create an intermediate stock to ensure that the factory can respond to the demands of the distributor. You will also probably hold raw material stock so that you do not have to wait for supplies every time you start to make something.

Time Scenarios

#12 Simple Factory: Inventory, Response & Lead Time

This is the same operation as before

Response Time and Lead Time outputs are now investigated.

Predicted output and difference tables are added to cost and inventory.

The inputs already in use provide the data that is needed. We also need to visualise the routings ("what parts go into what other parts") in order to work out the answers.

Predicted Values

250,000 items/yr

COST		Material	Other	per item
	VOLUME	$417,781	$317,513	$2.941
	BATCH		$7,620	$0.030
	PRODUCT		$0	$0.000
	FACILITY		$280,000	$1.120
	TOTAL		**$1,022,914**	**$4.09**

INVENTORY	Material only	ML&O
Raw Material	$24,037	$24,000
WIP	$12,285	$30,100
Finished	$0	$0
All	**$36,322**	**$54,100**

RESPONSE TIME		LEAD TIME	
All-in-one process	**13** days	**11** days	

Process Description

Task ref	Activity	Qty per sale	unit	Run waste	Fixed Batch waste	Batch size	Batches per Year	Same Batches per Year as other task?
1	All-in-one process	1	pack	15%	300	2,500		

Variable Cost Inputs

Task ref	Activity	Items per Minute	Batch Change over Hours	Manning	Non Value Adding Hours per Hour	Labor Rate per Hour	Employer Costs per Hour	Material Value Added
1	All-in-one process	2	0.5	3	1.0	$15.00	$4.00	$1.25

12

Questions:
What change to a Response Time, Lead Time & Inventory input causes this increase in Lead Time?

Why does Response Time also increase by this much?

Hints:
Figure out if the WIP increase is due to In Process or Intermediate inventory. Look again at the definition of Response Time.

Answers at www.BridgeoFaith.com

Differences

Cost Change	Material	Other	per item
VOLUME	$0	$0	$0.000
BATCH		$0	$0.000
PRODUCT		$0	$0.000
FACILITY		$0	$0.000
TOTAL		$0	$0.000

Inventory Change	Material only	ML&O
Raw Material	$0	$0
WIP	$8,012	$19,600
Finished	$0	$0
All	$8,012	$19,600

Response Time Change		Lead Time Change	
All-in-one process	7 days	7	days

Response Time, Lead Time & Inventory Inputs

Task ref	Varieties	RM Min Days Stock	RM Days between Deliveries	Intermed Days Hold Time	Intermed Days Min Sawtooth	Finished Goods Days Hold Time	Finished Goods Days Min Stock
1	1	14	14				

#13 Simple Factory: Cost, Inventory and Time

This is still the operation of the previous exercises.

We now look at the impact of an input that affects inventory and time as well as cost.

Predicted Values   250,000 items/yr

COST	Material	Other	per item
VOLUME	$417,781	$158,757	$2.306
BATCH		$7,620	$0.030
PRODUCT		$0	$0.000
FACILITY		$280,000	$1.120
TOTAL		**$864,158**	**$3.46**

INVENTORY	Material only	ML&O
Raw Material	$24,037	$24,000
WIP	$2,187	$4,500
Finished	$0	$0
All	**$26,223**	**$28,500**

RESPONSE TIME		LEAD TIME	
All-in-one process	**5** days	**2** days	

Process Description

Task ref	Activity	Qty per sale	unit	Run waste	Fixed Batch waste	Batch size	Batches per Year	Same Batches per Year as other task?
1	All-in-one process	1	pack	15%	300	2,500		

Variable Cost Inputs

Task ref	Activity	Items per Minute	Batch Change over Hours	Manning	Non Value Adding Hours per Hour	Labor Rate per Hour	Employer Costs per Hour	Material Value Added
1	All-in-one process	2	0.5	3	1.0	$15.00	$4.00	$1.25

13

Question:
What change to a single Cost input reduces Lead Time by 2 days?

Hint:
Look first for the cost input that creates the cost difference shown. Then work out how this affects WIP and then time.

Answer at www.BridgeoFaith.com

Differences

Cost Change	Material	Other	per item
VOLUME	$0	-$158,757	-$0.635
BATCH		$0	$0.000
PRODUCT		$0	$0.000
FACILITY		$0	$0.000
TOTAL	-$158,757		-$0.635

Inventory Change	Material only	ML&O
Raw Material	$0	$0
WIP	-$2,087	-$6,000
Finished	$0	$0
All	-$2,087	-$6,000

Response Time Change	Lead Time Change
All-in-one process -1.8 days	-1.8 days

Response Time, Lead Time & Inventory Inputs

Task ref	Varieties	RM Min Days Stock	RM Days between Deliveries	Intermed Days Hold Time	Intermed Days Min Sawtooth	Finished Goods Days Hold Time	Finished Goods Days Min Stock
1	1	14	14				

#14 Simple Factory: Cost, Inventory & Time

This is the same operation as before.

We are now trying to do our best to become more responsive. However, this is at a price.

There are also some inventory anomalies to resolve.

We ask you to consider whether you would consider a trade-off of one measure against another.

Answer at www.BridgeoFaith.com

Predicted Values

250,000 items/yr

COST	Material	Other	per item
VOLUME	$459,559	$349,265	$3.235
BATCH		$13,971	$0.056
PRODUCT		$0	$0.000
FACILITY		$280,000	$1.120
TOTAL	**$1,102,794**		**$4.41**

INVENTORY	Material only	ML&O
Raw Material	$26,440	$26,400
WIP	$2,864	$6,900
Finished	$0	$0
All	**$29,305**	**$33,300**

RESPONSE TIME		LEAD TIME	
All-in-one process	4 days	2 days	

Process Description

Task ref	Activity	Qty per sale	unit	Run waste	Fixed Batch waste	Batch size	Batches per Year	Same Batches per Year as other task?
1	All-in-one process	1	pack	15%	300	2,500		

Variable Cost Inputs

Task ref	Activity	Items per Minute	Batch Change over Hours	Manning	Non Value Adding Hours per Hour	Labor Rate per Hour	Employer Costs per Hour	Material Value Added
1	All-in-one process	2	0.5	3	1.0	$15.00	$4.00	$1.25

14

Questions:
1. What change to a Process input causes all these changes?
2. Why does Response Time reduce more than Lead Time?
3. Why does RM inventory go up, whilst WIP goes down?
4. How do you reconcile the fact that material inventory value increases, but ML&O inventory drops?
5. Would you make the change?

Hint:
Refer to exercise #11

Differences

Cost Change	Material	Other	per item
VOLUME	$41,778	$31,751	$0.294
BATCH		$6,350	$0.025
PRODUCT		$0	$0.000
FACILITY		$0	$0.000
TOTAL		$79,880	$0.320

Inventory Change	Material only	ML&O
Raw Material	$2,404	$2,400
WIP	-$1,409	-$3,600
Finished	$0	$0
All	$995	-$1,200

Response Time Change		Lead Time Change	
All-in-one process	**-3** days	**-1**	days

Response Time, Lead Time & Inventory Inputs

Task ref	Varieties	RM Min Days Stock	RM Days between Deliveries	Intermed Days Hold Time	Intermed Days Min Sawtooth	Finished Goods Days Hold Time	Finished Goods Days Min Stock
1	1	14	14				

5. CAPACITY

Calculation of Capacity Utilization

Capacity is calculated by comparing the hours needed to do all the anticipated work and comparing this with the hours available in each work center.

Capacity Utilization is equal to: $\dfrac{\text{Hours Needed}}{\text{Hours Available}}$

Hours needed includes short periods at the ends of shifts that cannot be used productively. You would not start something then, because you could not finish it.

Hours available includes the effect of downtime or when the line is not available for use.

$$= \frac{\text{Run hrs + Changeover hrs + Hrs unusable at end of Shift}}{\text{Shifts per week x Hours per Shift } - \text{ Hours per Week Not Available}}$$

An Example:

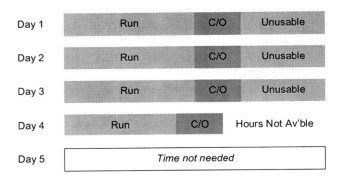

The reported utilization is 4 full days out of 5, i.e. 80%. Note that the line is only running productively for about 40% of the time. Other hours are needed for other things, as well as some that are not available at all.

Extra capacity can often be found by reducing changeover (C/O) time, changing shift pattern to eliminate unusable parts of the day, or increasing up time on the line.

Capacity Inputs

This is what the shop floor terms mean:

Work Center	Sometimes one work center is used for more than one activity. In this situation, capacity is used by both activities. For example a formulation area might be used for generics or special reagents.
Spell Hours	This is like a shift, but notes whether the shifts run immediately after each other. A double shift 0600–1400 + 1400–2200 would be a single spell of 16 hours. A long spell allows the production of large batches that cannot be stopped once started.
Spells per week	The number of spells in a week. Note that 10 x 8 hours shifts as above would be 5 x 16 hours spells.
Number of Lines	The number of parallel routes in which the job could be done. Can be machines, work benches or even just people, for example QA releasing product.
Break Batch?	"Yes" indicates that the batch can be halted partly complete at the end of a spell, then resumed at a later time. When "Yes", no time is unusable at the end of a shift.
Hours/week not available	Time when a line cannot be used for setup or run. Includes general maintenance, breakdowns or time when there are no staff to keep the line running.

Capacity Scenarios

#15 Simple Factory: Capacity

This exercise introduces the last group of inputs and the Capacity output.

Let's look first at a change affecting capacity alone

Predicted Values

250,000 items/yr

COST		Material	Other	per item
	VOLUME	$417,781	$317,513	$2.941
	BATCH		$7,620	$0.030
	PRODUCT		$0	$0.000
	FACILITY		$280,000	$1.120
	TOTAL		**$1,022,914**	**$4.09**

INVENTORY	Material only	ML&O
Raw Material	$24,037	$24,000
WIP	$4,273	$10,500
Finished	$9,575	$23,400
All	**$37,885**	**$57,900**

RESPONSE TIME		LEAD TIME	
All-in-one process	**6** days	**4** days	

CAPACITY	Most Used WorkCenter		
	Assembly area	**79%**	Utilization

Process Description

Task ref	Activity	Qty per sale	unit	Run waste	Fixed Batch waste	Batch size	Batches per Year	Same Batches per Year as other task?
1	All-in-one process	1	pack	15%	300	2,500		

Variable Cost Inputs

Task ref	Activity	Items per Minute	Batch Change over Hours	Manning	Non Value Adding Hours per Hour	Labor Rate per Hour	Employer Costs per Hour	Material Value Added
1	All-in-one process	2	0.5	3	1.0	$15.00	$4.00	$1.25

15

Question:
Which Capacity input would cause the change shown in the difference table?

How much has it changed?

Hints:
The definition of Capacity Utilization includes factors other than shift pattern.
Avoid factors that affect WIP.

Answer at www.BridgeoFaith.com

Differences

Cost Change	Material	Other	per item
VOLUME	$0	$0	$0.000
BATCH		$0	$0.000
PRODUCT		$0	$0.000
FACILITY		$0	$0.000
TOTAL		$0	$0.000

Inventory Change	Material only	ML&O
Raw Material	$0	$0
WIP	$0	$0
Finished	$0	$0
All	$0	$0

Response Time Change		Lead Time Change	
All-in-one process	0 days	0	days

Capacity Change	Old Most Used W/C		
	Assembly area	10%	Utilization Difference

Capacity Inputs

Task ref	Work Center	Spell Hours	Spells per Week	Number of Lines	Break Batch?	Hours per Wk not Available
1	Assembly area	8	5	2	Yes	

Response Time, Lead Time & Inventory Inputs

Task ref	Varieties	RM Min Days Stock	RM Days between Deliveries	Intermed Days Hold Time	Intermed Days Min Sawtooth	Finished Goods Days Hold Time	Finished Goods Days Min Stock
1	1	14	14				7

#16 Simple Factory: Capacity

This is still the same operation of the previous exercises.

This time a simple change also has an impact on inventory, response time and lead time.

Predicted Values   250,000 items/yr

COST	Material	Other	per item
VOLUME	$417,781	$317,513	$2.941
BATCH		$7,620	$0.030
PRODUCT		$0	$0.000
FACILITY		$280,000	$1.120
TOTAL		**$1,022,914**	**$4.09**

INVENTORY	Material only	ML&O
Raw Material	$24,037	$24,000
WIP	$2,137	$5,200
Finished	$9,575	$23,400
All	**$35,748**	**$52,600**

RESPONSE TIME		LEAD TIME	
All-in-one process	**5** days	**2** days	

CAPACITY	Most Used WorkCenter		
	Assembly area	**34%**	Utilization

Process Description

Task ref	Activity	Qty per sale	unit	Run waste	Fixed Batch waste	Batch size	Batches per Year	Same Batches per Year as other task?
1	All-in-one process	1	pack	15%	300	2,500		

Variable Cost Inputs

Task ref	Activity	Items per Minute	Batch Change over Hours	Manning	Non Value Adding Hours per Hour	Labor Rate per Hour	Employer Costs per Hour	Material Value Added
1	All-in-one process	2	0.5	3	1.0	$15.00	$4.00	$1.25

16

Questions:
Which Capacity input would cause the change to Capacity Utilization shown in the difference table?

Why have Response Time, Lead Time and WIP reduced?

Hint:
Work out how long it takes to process a batch.

Answer at www.BridgeoFaith.com

Differences

Cost Change	Material	Other	per item
VOLUME	$0	$0	$0.000
BATCH		$0	$0.000
PRODUCT		$0	$0.000
FACILITY		$0	$0.000
TOTAL	$0	$0	$0.000

Inventory Change	Material only	ML&O
Raw Material	$0	$0
WIP	-$2,137	-$5,300
Finished	$0	$0
All	-$2,137	-$5,300

Response Time Change		Lead Time Change	
All-in-one process	**-2** days	**-2**	days

Capacity Change	Old Most Used W/C		
	Assembly area	**-34%**	Utilization Difference

Capacity Inputs

Task ref	Work Center	Spell Hours	Spells per Week	Number of Lines	Break Batch?	Hours per Week not Available
1	Assembly area	8	5	2	Yes	

Response Time, Lead Time & Inventory Inputs

Task ref	Varieties	RM Min Days Stock	RM Days between Deliveries	Intermed Days Hold Time	Intermed Days Min Sawtooth	Finished Goods Days Hold Time	Finished Goods Days Min Stock
1	1	14	14				7

#17 Simple Factory: Capacity

This exercise builds on the previous one.

That provided lots of spare capacity. This is not needed, so there is freedom to reduce it.

A total of 2 changes cause the effect seen.

Predicted Values

250,000 items/yr

COST	Material	Other	per item
VOLUME	$417,781	$317,513	$2.941
BATCH		$7,620	$0.030
PRODUCT		$0	$0.000
FACILITY		$280,000	$1.120
TOTAL		**$1,022,914**	**$4.09**

INVENTORY	Material only	ML&O
Raw Material	$24,037	$24,000
WIP	$2,137	$5,200
Finished	$9,575	$23,400
All	**$35,748**	**$52,600**

RESPONSE TIME		LEAD TIME	
All-in-one process	**5** days	**2** days	

CAPACITY	Most Used WorkCenter		
	Assembly area	**69%**	Utilization

Process Description

Task ref	Activity	Qty per sale	unit	Run waste	Fixed Batch waste	Batch size	Batches per Year	Same Batches per Year as other task?
1	All-in-one process	1	pack	15%	300	2,500		

Variable Cost Inputs

Task ref	Activity	Items per Minute	Batch Change over Hours	Manning	Non Value Adding Hours per Hour	Labor Rate per Hour	Employer Costs per Hour	Material Value Added
1	All-in-one process	2	0.5	3	1.0	$15.00	$4.00	$1.25

17

Question:
Which Capacity input additional to that changed in the previous example would bring the Capacity Utilization back to its former level, but leave Response Time, Lead Time and WIP improved?

Hint:
Look at how much the capacity utilization changed.

Answer at www.BridgeoFaith.com

Differences

Cost Change	Material	Other	per item
VOLUME	$0	$0	$0.000
BATCH		$0	$0.000
PRODUCT		$0	$0.000
FACILITY		$0	$0.000
TOTAL		$0	$0.000

Inventory Change	Material only	ML&O
Raw Material	$0	$0
WIP	-$2,137	-$5,300
Finished	$0	$0
All	-$2,137	-$5,300

Response Time Change		Lead Time Change	
All-in-one process	**-2** days	**-2**	days

Capacity	Old Most Used W/C		
Change	Assembly area	0%	Utilization Difference

Capacity Inputs

Task ref	Work Center	Spell Hours	Spells per Week	Number of Lines	Break Batch?	Hours per Wk not Available
1	Assembly area	8	5	2	Yes	

Response Time, Lead Time & Inventory Inputs

Task ref	Varieties	RM Min Days Stock	RM Days between Deliveries	Intermed Days Hold Time	Intermed Days Min Sawtooth	Finished Goods Days Hold Time	Finished Goods Days Min Stock
1	1	14	14				7

"Habit is habit,
and not to be flung out of the window by any man
but coaxed downstairs a step at a time."

Mark Twain

6. ALL MEASURES

We will see that it is hard to find a change that does not have an impact on something other than the desired one.

Scenario 18 thru 20 explore further the single step operation of all previous examples.

Scenarios 21 thru 25 add a second process step.

#18 Simple Factory: All Measures

This is still the operation of the previous exercises.

The last couple of exercises looked specifically at capacity. We saw that it is hard to alter capacity without affecting other measures.

We now look at all kind of change that may affect any or all business measures of cost, inventory, time and capacity.

Predicted Values
250,000 items/yr

COST

	Material	Other	per item
VOLUME	$459,559	$349,265	$3.235
BATCH		$13,971	$0.056
PRODUCT		$0	$0.000
FACILITY		$280,000	$1.120
TOTAL		**$1,102,794**	**$4.41**

INVENTORY

	Material only	ML&O
Raw Material	$26,440	$26,400
WIP	$2,864	$6,900
Finished	$0	$0
All	**$29,305**	**$33,300**

RESPONSE TIME / LEAD TIME

RESPONSE TIME		LEAD TIME	
All-in-one process	**4** days	**2** days	

CAPACITY

CAPACITY	Most Used WorkCenter Utilization
	Assembly area **77%**

Process Description

Task ref	Activity	Qty per sale	unit	Run waste	Fixed Batch waste	Batch size	Batches per Year	Same Batches per Year as other task?
1	All-in-one process	1	pack	15%	300	2,500		

Variable Cost Inputs

Task ref	Activity	Items per Minute	Batch Change over Hours	Manning	Non Value Adding Hours per Hour	Labor Rate per Hour	Employer Costs per Hour	Material Value Added
1	All-in-one process	2	0.5	3	1.0	$15.00	$4.00	$1.25

18

Question:
Which Process change would cause all the differences shown above?

Hint:
Look at exercise #14.

Answer at www.BridgeoFaith.com

Differences

Cost Change	Material	Other	per item
VOLUME	$41,778	$31,751	$0.294
BATCH		$6,350	$0.025
PRODUCT		$0	$0.000
FACILITY		$0	$0.000
TOTAL		$79,880	$0.320

Inventory Change	Material only	ML&O
Raw Material	$2,404	$2,400
WIP	-$1,409	-$3,600
Finished	$0	$0
All	$995	-$1,200

Response Time Change		Lead Time Change	
All-in-one process	**-3** days	**-1**	days

Capacity Change	Old Most Used W/C	Utilization Difference
	Assembly area	**8%**

Capacity Inputs

Task ref	Work Center	Spell Hours	Spells per Week	Number of Lines	Break Batch?	Hours per Wk not Available
1	Assembly area	8	5	2	Yes	

Response Time, Lead Time & Inventory Inputs

Task ref	Varieties	RM Min Days Stock	RM Days between Deliveries	Intermed Days Hold Time	Intermed Days Min Sawtooth	Finished Goods Days Hold Time	Finished Goods Days Min Stock
1	1	14	14				

#19 Simple Factory: All Measures

This scenario builds on the change of the last.

Reducing response time is great from the customer's point of view, but nobody in the business wants it to cost more.

Including the last, a total of 2 shop floor changes creates the effect shown.

The result is a lower cost, more responsive operation with capacity to spare.

Predicted Values

250,000 items/yr

COST	Material	Other	per item
VOLUME	$459,559	$232,843	$2.770
BATCH		$13,971	$0.056
PRODUCT		$0	$0.000
FACILITY		$280,000	$1.120
TOTAL		**$986,373**	**$3.95**

INVENTORY	Material only	ML&O
Raw Material	$26,440	$26,400
WIP	$1,946	$4,200
Finished	$9,751	$20,900
All	**$38,138**	**$51,500**

RESPONSE TIME		LEAD TIME	
All-in-one process	**3** days	**2** days	

CAPACITY	Most Used WorkCenter		
	Assembly area	**52%**	Utilization

Process Description

Task ref	Activity	Qty per sale	unit	Run waste	Fixed Batch waste	Batch size	Batches per Year	Same Batches per Year as other task?
1	All-in-one process	1	pack	15%	300	1,500		

Variable Cost Inputs

Task ref	Activity	Items per Minute	Batch Change over Hours	Manning	Non Value Adding Hours per Hour	Labor Rate per Hour	Employer Costs per Hour	Material Value Added
1	All-in-one process	2	0.5	3	1.0	$15.00	$4.00	$1.25

19

Question:
Which Cost input change as well as the Process change of the previous example would cause all the differences shown above?

Hint:
The cost saving is with volume related labor

Answer at www.BridgeoFaith.com

Differences

Cost Change	Material	Other	per item
VOLUME	$41,778	-$84,670	-$0.172
BATCH		$6,350	$0.025
PRODUCT		$0	$0.000
FACILITY		$0	$0.000
TOTAL		-$36,542	-$0.146

Inventory Change	Material only	ML&O
Raw Material	$2,404	$2,400
WIP	-$2,327	-$6,300
Finished	$176	-$2,500
All	$253	-$6,400

Response Time Change		Lead Time Change	
All-in-one process	**-3** days	**-2**	days

Capacity Change	Old Most Used W/C		
	Assembly area	**-17%**	Utilization Difference

Capacity Inputs

Task ref	Work Center	Spell Hours	Spells per Week	Number of Lines	Break Batch?	Hours per Week not Available
1	Assembly area	8	5	2	Yes	

Response Time, Lead Time & Inventory Inputs

Task ref	Varieties	RM Min Days Stock	RM Days between Deliveries	Intermed Days Hold Time	Intermed Days Min Sawtooth	Finished Goods Days Hold Time	Finished Goods Days Min Stock
1	1	14	14				7

#20 Simple Factory: All Measures

This is still the operation of the previous scenarios.

Here the change is not initiated by the shop floor.

Nevertheless, there is a worsening of most of the business measures.

Predicted Values

250,000 items/yr

COST	Material	Other	per item
VOLUME	$417,781	$317,513	$2.941
BATCH		$7,620	$0.030
PRODUCT		$70,000	$0.280
FACILITY		$210,000	$0.840
TOTAL		**$1,022,914**	**$4.09**

INVENTORY	Material only	ML&O
Raw Material	$24,037	$24,000
WIP	$4,273	$10,500
Finished	$11,137	$27,300
All	**$39,447**	**$61,800**

RESPONSE TIME		LEAD TIME	
All-in-one process	**9** days	**4** days	

CAPACITY	Most Used WorkCenter Utilization	
	Assembly area	**69%**

Process Description

Task ref	Activity	Qty per sale	unit	Run waste	Fixed Batch waste	Batch size	Batches per Year	Same Batches per Year as other task?
1	All-in-one process	1	pack	15%	300	2,500		

Variable Cost Inputs

Task ref	Activity	Items per Minute	Batch Change over Hours	Manning	Non Value Adding Hours per Hour	Labor Rate per Hour	Employer Costs per Hour	Material Value Added
1	All-in-one process	2	0.5	3	1.0	$15.00	$4.00	$1.25

Questions:

Changing which input causes everything to change except Capacity Utilization and Lead Time?

What is going on?

Hints:

Look at where the cost difference occurs.
What have marketing done?

Answer at www.BridgeoFaith.com

Differences

Cost Change

Cost Change	Material	Other	per item
VOLUME	$0	$0	$0.000
BATCH		$0	$0.000
PRODUCT		$35,000	$0.140
FACILITY		$0	$0.000
TOTAL		$35,000	$0.140

Inventory Change	Material only	ML&O
Raw Material	$0	$0
WIP	$0	$400
Finished	$1,563	$4,700
All	$1,563	$5,100

Response Time Change		Lead Time Change	
All-in-one process	3 days	0	days

Capacity Change	Old Most Used W/C	Utilization Difference
	Assembly area	0%

Capacity Inputs

Task ref	Work Center	Spell Hours	Spells per Week	Number of Lines	Break Batch?	Hours per Wk not Available
1	Assembly area	8	5	2	Yes	

Response Time, Lead Time & Inventory Inputs

Task ref	Varieties	RM Min Days Stock	RM Days between Deliveries	Intermed Days Hold Time	Intermed Days Min Sawtooth	Finished Goods Days Hold Time	Finished Goods Days Min Stock
1	1	14	14				7

#20

85   www.BridgeoFaith.com

#21 Operation with 2 Process Steps

This is a new operation defined in 2 steps.

The first step is making components
The second step is assembly.

The style of the business outputs is as before, while the extra process step adds another row to each input table.

The batch size policy is a fixed batch frequency (roughly every week) with assembly done at the same time.

Predicted Values

250,000 items/yr

COST	Material	Other	per item
VOLUME	$182,056	$137,134	$1.277
BATCH		$9,500	$0.038
PRODUCT		$28,000	$0.112
FACILITY		$252,000	$1.008
TOTAL		**$608,690**	**$2.43**

INVENTORY	Material only	ML&O
Raw Material	$11,786	$11,800
WIP	$1,279	$4,300
Finished	$3,662	$12,200
All	**$16,727**	**$28,300**

RESPONSE TIME		LEAD TIME
Assembly	**11** days	**4** days

CAPACITY	Most Used WorkCenter
	Assembly area **53%** Utilized

Process Description

Task ref	Activity	Qty per sale	unit	Run waste	Fixed Batch waste	Batch size	Batches per Year	Same Batches per Year as other task?
1	Make components	2	part	10%	100		50	
2	Assembly	1	pack		10			1

Variable Cost Inputs

Task ref	Activity	Items per Minute	Batch Change over Hours	Manning	Non Value Adding Hours per Hour	Labor Rate per Hour	Employer Costs per Hour	Material Value Added
1	Make components	20	1.0	1	1.0	$15.00	$4.00	$0.10
2	Assembly	4	0.5	3	1.0	$15.00	$4.00	$0.50

21

Question:
What Process change would cause the changes shown in the difference table?

Hint:
Compare the largest cost change with the response time change.

Answer at www.BridgeoFaith.com

Differences

Cost Change	Material	Other	per item
VOLUME	$750	$396	$0.005
BATCH		$4,750	$0.019
PRODUCT		$0	$0.000
FACILITY		$0	$0.000
TOTAL		$5,896	$0.024

Inventory Change	Material only	ML&O
Raw Material	$71	$100
WIP	-$868	-$2,800
Finished	-$1,245	-$4,100
All	-$2,042	-$6,800

Response Time Change		Lead Time Change	
Assembly	-10 days	-3	days

Capacity Change	Old Most Used W/C		
	Assembly area	1%	Utilization Difference

Capacity Inputs

Task ref	Work Center	Spell Hours	Spells per Week	Number of Lines	Break Batch?	Hours per Week not Available
1	Component area	8	5	1	Yes	
2	Assembly area	8	5	1	Yes	

Response Time, Lead Time & Inventory Inputs

Task ref	Varieties	RM Min Days Stock	RM Days between Deliveries	Intermed Days Hold Time	Intermed Days Min Sawtooth	Finished Goods Days Hold Time	Finished Goods Days Min Stock
1	2	30	30	1			
2	2	7	14				7

#22 Operation with 2 Process Steps

Another look at the 2 step operation of the last scenario.

This scenario looks at one aspect of "lean" thinking.

The effect is only on cost, and the fully burdened inventory change is simply a reflection of that.

Predicted Values

250,000 items/yr

COST	Material	Other	per item
VOLUME	$181,306	$102,554	$1.135
BATCH		$3,563	$0.014
PRODUCT		$28,000	$0.112
FACILITY		$252,000	$1.008
TOTAL		**$567,422**	**$2.27**

INVENTORY	Material only	ML&O
Raw Material	$11,715	$11,700
WIP	$2,147	$6,700
Finished	$4,907	$15,400
All	**$18,769**	**$33,800**

RESPONSE TIME		LEAD TIME	
Assembly	**21** days	**7** days	

CAPACITY	Most Used WorkCenter		
	Assembly area	**51%**	Utilized

Process Description

Task ref	Activity	Qty per sale	unit	Run waste	Fixed Batch waste	Batch size	Batches per Year	Same Batches per Year as other task?
1	Make components	2	part	10%	100		50	
2	Assembly	1	pack		10			1

Variable Cost Inputs

Task ref	Activity	Items per Minute	Batch Change over Hours	Manning	Non Value Adding Hours per Hour	Labor Rate per Hour	Employer Costs per Hour	Material Value Added
1	Make components	20	1.0	1	1.0	$15.00	$4.00	$0.10
2	Assembly	4	0.5	3	1.0	$15.00	$4.00	$0.50

22

Questions:
Which 2 Cost inputs would cause the changes shown in the difference table?
How much did they change?

Hint:
The labor cost change (right output table) is in proportion to the volume and batch related cost (left output table)

Answer at www.BridgeoFaith.com

Differences

Cost Change	Material	Other	per item
VOLUME	$0	-$34,185	-$0.137
BATCH		-$1,188	-$0.005
PRODUCT		$0	$0.000
FACILITY		$0	$0.000
TOTAL		-$35,372	-$0.141

Inventory Change	Material only	ML&O
Raw Material	$0	$0
WIP	$0	-$400
Finished	$0	-$900
All	$0	-$1,300

Response Time Change	Lead Time Change
Assembly 0 days	0 days

Capacity Change	Old Most Used W/C
	Assembly area 0% Utilization Difference

Capacity Inputs

Task ref	Work Center	Spell Hours	Spells per Week	Number of Lines	Break Batch?	Hours per Week not Available
1	Component area	8	5	1	Yes	
2	Assembly area	8	5	1	Yes	

Response Time, Lead Time & Inventory Inputs

Task ref	Varieties	RM Min Days Stock	RM Days between Deliveries	Intermed Days Hold Time	Intermed Days Min Sawtooth	Finished Goods Days Hold Time	Finished Goods Days Min Stock
1	2	30	30	1			
2	2	7	14				7

#23 Operation with 2 Process Steps

Another scenario with the 2 step operation.

This starts with the change of scenario #22 and adds a further improvement.

Predicted Values

250,000 items/yr

COST	Material	Other	per item
VOLUME	$181,306	$102,554	$1.135
BATCH		$3,563	$0.014
PRODUCT		$28,000	$0.112
FACILITY		$252,000	$1.008
TOTAL		$567,422	$2.27

INVENTORY	Material only	ML&O
Raw Material	$11,715	$11,700
WIP	$1,840	$5,800
Finished	$4,907	$15,400
All	$18,462	$32,900

RESPONSE TIME		LEAD TIME
Assembly	20 days	6 days

CAPACITY	Most Used WorkCenter
	Assembly area 51% Utilized

Process Description

Task ref	Activity	Qty per sale	unit	Run waste	Fixed Batch waste	Batch size	Batches per Year	Same Batches Year as other task?
1	Make components	2	part	10%	100		50	
2	Assembly	1	pack		10			1

Variable Cost Inputs

Task ref	Activity	Items per Minute	Batch Change over Hours	Manning	Non Value Adding Hours per Hour	Labor Rate per Hour	Employer Costs per Hour	Material Value Added
1	Make components	20	1.0	1	1.0	$15.00	$4.00	$0.10
2	Assembly	4	0.5	3	1.0	$15.00	$4.00	$0.50

23

Questions:
Which Time & Inventory input additional to the Cost input change of the previous example would cause the change shown in the difference table?
How much did it change?

Hint:
WIP changed but cost did not.

Answer at www.BridgeoFaith.com

Differences

Cost Change	Material	Other	per item
VOLUME	$0	-$34,185	-$0.137
BATCH		-$1,188	-$0.005
PRODUCT		$0	$0.000
FACILITY		$0	$0.000
TOTAL		**-$35,372**	**-$0.141**

Inventory Change	Material only	ML&O
Raw Material	$0	$0
WIP	-$307	-$1,300
Finished	$0	-$900
All	**-$307**	**-$2,200**

Response Time Change		Lead Time Change	
Assembly	**-1** days	**-1**	days

Capacity Change	Old Most Used W/C		
	Assembly area	0%	Utilization Difference

Capacity Inputs

Task ref	Work Center	Spell Hours	Spells per Week	Number of Lines	Break Batch?	Hours per Week not Available
1	Component area	8	5	1	Yes	
2	Assembly area	8	5	1	Yes	

Response Time, Lead Time & Inventory Inputs

Task ref	Varieties	RM Min Days Stock	RM Days between Deliveries	Intermed Days Hold Time	Intermed Days Min Sawtooth	Finished Goods Days Hold Time	Finished Goods Days Min Stock
1	2	30	30	1			
2	2	7	14				7

#24 Operation with 2 Process Steps

The same 2 step operation.

This is a classic way to improve Responsiveness.

Predicted Values

250,000 items/yr

COST		Material	Other	per item
	VOLUME	$182,056	$137,451	$1.278
	BATCH		$13,300	$0.053
	PRODUCT		$28,000	$0.112
	FACILITY		$252,000	$1.008
	TOTAL		**$612,806**	**$2.45**

INVENTORY	Material only	ML&O
Raw Material	$11,744	$11,700
WIP	$3,453	$11,600
Finished	$3,046	$10,300
All	**$18,243**	**$33,600**

RESPONSE TIME		LEAD TIME	
Assembly	**5** days	**1** days	

CAPACITY	Most Used WorkCenter		
	Assembly area	**55%**	Utilized

Process Description

Task ref	Activity	Qty per sale	unit	Run waste	Fixed Batch waste	Batch size	Batches per Year	Same Batches per Year as other task?
1	Make components	2	part	10%	100		50	
2	Assembly	1	pack		10			1

Variable Cost Inputs

Task ref	Activity	Items per Minute	Batch Change over Hours	Manning	Non Value Adding Hours per Hour	Labor Rate per Hour	Employer Costs per Hour	Material Value Added
1	Make components	20	1.0	1	1.0	$15.00	$4.00	$0.10
2	Assembly	4	0.5	3	1.0	$15.00	$4.00	$0.50

24

Questions:
Which Process inputs would cause the changes shown in the difference table?
Why did Response Time improve so dramatically?

Hint:
Ask yourself why batch related cost went up, but not as much as it might have.

Answer at www.BridgeoFaith.com

Differences

Cost Change	Material	Other	per item
VOLUME	$750	$713	$0.006
BATCH		$8,550	$0.034
PRODUCT		$0	$0.000
FACILITY		$0	$0.000
TOTAL		$10,013	$0.040

Inventory Change	Material only	ML&O
Raw Material	$29	$0
WIP	$1,306	$4,500
Finished	-$1,861	-$6,000
All	-$526	-$1,500

Response Time Change		Lead Time Change	
Assembly	-16 days	-6	days

Capacity Change	Old Most Used W/C		
	Assembly area	4%	Utilization Difference

Capacity Inputs

Task ref	Work Center	Spell Hours	Spells per Week	Number of Lines	Break Batch?	Hours per Week not Available
1	Component area	8	5	1	Yes	
2	Assembly area	8	5	1	Yes	

Response Time, Lead Time & Inventory Inputs

Task ref	Varieties	RM Min Days Stock	RM Days between Deliveries	Intermed Days Hold Time	Intermed Days Min Sawtooth	Finished Goods Days Hold Time	Finished Goods Days Min Stock
1	2	30	30	1			
2	2	7	14				7

#25 Operation with 2 Process Steps

Sceanrio #24 vastly improved responsiveness, but at a cost.

This exercise consolidates the change of #24 with something extra to save that money.

It does it in a slightly surprising way!

Predicted Values

250,000 items/yr

COST	Material	Other	per item
VOLUME	$182,056	$124,151	$1.225
BATCH		$9,500	$0.038
PRODUCT		$28,000	$0.112
FACILITY		$252,000	$1.008
TOTAL		**$595,706**	**$2.38**

INVENTORY	Material only	ML&O
Raw Material	$11,744	$11,700
WIP	$3,559	$11,600
Finished	$3,046	$10,000
All	**$18,349**	**$33,300**

RESPONSE TIME		LEAD TIME	
Assembly	**5** days	**1** days	

CAPACITY	Most Used WorkCenter		
	Assembly area	**72%**	Utilized

Process Description

Task ref	Activity	Qty per sale	unit	Run waste	Fixed Batch waste	Batch size	Batches per Year	Same Batches per Year as other task?
1	Make components	2	part	10%	100		50	
2	Assembly	1	pack		10			1

Variable Cost Inputs

Task ref	Activity	Items per Minute	Batch Change over Hours	Manning	Non Value Adding Hours per Hour	Labor Rate per Hour	Employer Costs per Hour	Material Value Added
1	Make components	20	1.0	1	1.0	$15.00	$4.00	$0.10
2	Assembly	4	0.5	3	1.0	$15.00	$4.00	$0.50

25

Question:
Starting from the change made in the previous example, what 2 additional Variable Cost changes would ensure that there was a net cost saving?

Hint:
There is now an increase in assembly area utilization, and a reduced batch related difference.

Answer at www.BridgeoFaith.com

Differences

Cost Change	Material	Other	per item
VOLUME	$750	-$12,588	-$0.047
BATCH		$4,750	$0.019
PRODUCT		$0	$0.000
FACILITY		$0	$0.000
TOTAL		-$7,088	-$0.028

Inventory Change	Material only	ML&O
Raw Material	$29	$0
WIP	$1,412	$4,500
Finished	-$1,861	-$6,300
All	-$420	-$1,800

Response Time Change		Lead Time Change	
Assembly	-16 days	-5	days

Capacity Change	Old Most Used W/C		
	Assembly area	21%	Utilization Difference

Capacity Inputs

Task ref	Work Center	Spell Hours	Spells per Week	Number of Lines	Break Batch?	Hours per Week not Available
1	Component area	8	5	1	Yes	
2	Assembly area	8	5	1	Yes	

Response Time, Lead Time & Inventory Inputs

Task ref	Varieties	RM Min Days Stock	RM Days between Deliveries	Intermed Days Hold Time	Intermed Days Min Sawtooth	Finished Goods Days Hold Time	Finished Goods Days Min Stock
1	2	30	30	1			
2	2	7	14				7

It's not so much that we're afraid of change or so in love with the old ways, but it's that place in between that we fear...It's like being between trapezes. It's Linus when his blanket is in the dryer. There's nothing to hold on to.

Marilyn Ferguson, U.S. futurist

7. Medical Device and Diagnostic Operations

Scenarios 26 to 35 discuss more elaborate and realistic operations.

They draw on experience in the medical device and diagnostic industry. In this business there are two issues that make their operations different:

1. Everybody thinks in terms of batches, including the regulators such as the FDA.

2. Non-production people tend to be involved, for example: troubleshooting, technical support, customer support, quality assurance. These people do not handle product, but their input is important to the operation.

There are 2 scenarios for each of:

• Specialist Reagents	#26 & 27
• Reagent Kit Factory	#28 & 29
• Point of Use Diagnostic Test	#30 & 31
• Single Use Pharmaceutical Product	#32 & 33
• Body Fluid Testing Kit	#34 & 35

The last one is discussed in more depth in the next chapter.

Specialist Reagents

First, a factory that makes a whole range of specialist chemicals that are formulated, tested, bottled and packed into boxes. They are all made to tight specifications in a regulated environment.

Scenarios 26 and 27 investigate.

#26 Specialist Reagents

Predicted Values

3,080,000 items/yr

COST	Material	Other	per item
VOLUME	$1,033,265	$318,377	$0.439
BATCH		$304,567	$0.099
PRODUCT		$435,000	$0.141
FACILITY		$892,500	$0.290
TOTAL	**$2,983,710**		**$0.969**

INVENTORY	Material only	ML&O
Raw Material	$120,365	$120,400
WIP	$17,747	$51,200
Finished	$153,991	$444,700
All	**$292,104**	**$616,300**

RESPONSE TIME		LEAD TIME
Pack	**92** days	**11** days

CAPACITY	Most Used WorkCentre		
	Customer Support	**79%**	Utilisation

Process Description

Task ref	Activity	Qty per sale	unit	Run waste	Fixed Batch waste	Batch size	Batch per Year	Same Batches/ Yr as other task?
1	Formulate reagent	1.00	bottle		300		64	
2	Test bulk		batch					1
3	Bottle	1.00	bottle	2%				1
4	Test		batch					1
5	Pack	0.07	pack		15			1
6	Customer support	1.00	batch					1
7	Technical support		batch					1
8	QA		batch					1

Variable Cost Inputs

Task ref	Activity	Items per Minute	Batch Change over Hours	Manning	Non Value Adding Hours per Hour	Labour Rate per Hour	Employer Costs per Hour	Material Value Added
1	Formulate reagent		5.0	2	2.0	$20.00	$8.00	$0.04
2	Test bulk		4.0	1	2.0	$25.00	$9.00	
3	Bottle	64.1	0.8	4	1.0	$20.00	$8.00	$0.17
4	Test		7.0	1	2.0	$30.00	$9.00	
5	Pack	4.8	0.3	3	0.5	$20.00	$8.00	$1.64
6	Customer support	68.4	11.7	1		$40.00	$10.00	
7	Technical support	35.2		1		$40.00	$10.00	
8	QA		4.4	1		$42.00	$11.00	

Changing which 2 of the inputs would lead to the
differences indicated below? How much have they
changed?

Differences

Cost Change	Material	Other	per item
VOLUME	$482	$84	$0.000
BATCH		-$5,489	-$0.002
PRODUCT		$0	$0.000
FACILITY		$0	$0.000
TOTAL		-$4,923	-$0.002

Inventory Change	Material only	ML&O
Raw Material	$59	$100
WIP	-$1,378	-$4,100
Finished	-$22,789	-$66,900
All	-$24,108	-$70,900

Response Time Change	Lead Time Change
Pack -17 days	-1 days

Capacity Change	Old Most Used W/C		
	Customer Support	7%	Utilisation Difference

Capacity Inputs

Task ref	Work Centre	Spell Hours	Spells per Week	Number of Lines	Break Batch?	Hours per Wk not Available
1	Formulations	8	5	1		4
2	QC	8	5	1		
3	Filling	14	5	1		4
4	QC	8	5	1		
5	Packing	8	5	1	Yes	
6	Customer Support	8	5	1	Yes	
7	TS	8	5	2	Yes	
8	QA	8	5	1		

Response Time, Lead Time & Inventory Inputs

Task ref	Varieties	RM Min Days Stock	RM Days between Deliveries	Intermed Days Hold Time	Intermed Days Min Sawtooth	Finished Goods Days Hold Time	Finished Goods Days Min Stock
1	17	60	60				
2	17			1			
3	17	30	30				
4	17			4			
5	17	14	14				14
6	17						
7	17						
8	17						

#27 Specialist Reagents

This is an attempt to save money, with little consideration for any other issue. Note that an activity that is not "production" (customer support) is key to this.

Predicted Values

3,080,000 items/yr

COST	Material	Other	per item
VOLUME	$1,032,784	$272,508	$0.424
BATCH		$307,368	$0.100
PRODUCT		$435,000	$0.141
FACILITY		$892,500	$0.290
TOTAL		**$2,940,159**	**$0.955**

INVENTORY	Material only	ML&O
Raw Material	$120,306	$120,300
WIP	$19,125	$54,400
Finished	$176,780	$503,300
All	**$316,212**	**$678,000**

RESPONSE TIME		LEAD TIME	
Pack	**108** days	**11** days	

CAPACITY	Most Used WorkCentre		
	Customer Support	**58%**	Utilisation

Process Description

Task ref	Activity	Qty per sale	unit	Run waste	Fixed Batch waste	Batch size	Batch per Year	Same Batches/ Yr as other task?
1	Formulate reagent	1.00	bottle		300		64	
2	Test bulk		batch					1
3	Bottle	1.00	bottle	2%				1
4	Test		batch					1
5	Pack	0.07	pack		15			1
6	Customer support	1.00	batch					1
7	Technical support		batch					1
8	QA		batch					1

Variable Cost Inputs

Task ref	Activity	Items per Minute	Batch Change over Hours	Manning	Non Value Adding Hours per Hour	Labour Rate per Hour	Employer Costs per Hour	Material Value Added
1	Formulate reagent		5.0	2	2.0	$20.00	$8.00	$0.04
2	Test bulk		4.0	1	2.0	$25.00	$9.00	
3	Bottle	64.1	0.8	4	1.0	$20.00	$8.00	$0.17
4	Test		7.0	1	2.0	$30.00	$9.00	
5	Pack	4.8	0.3	3	0.5	$20.00	$8.00	$1.64
6	Customer support	68.4	11.7	1		$40.00	$10.00	
7	Technical support	35.2		1		$40.00	$10.00	
8	QA		4.4	1		$42.00	$11.00	

Question:

Changing which 2 of the inputs would lead to the changes indicated below? How much have they changed?

Differences

Cost Change	Material	Other	per item
VOLUME	$0	-$45,786	-$0.015
BATCH		-$2,688	-$0.001
PRODUCT		$0	$0.000
FACILITY		$0	$0.000
TOTAL		-$48,474	-$0.016

Inventory Change	Material only	ML&O
Raw Material	$0	$0
WIP	$0	-$900
Finished	$0	-$8,300
All	$0	-$9,200

Response Time Change	Lead Time Change
Pack 0 days	0 days

Capacity Change	Old Most Used W/C		
	Customer Support	-14%	Utilisation Difference

Capacity Inputs

Task ref	Work Centre	Spell Hours	Spells per Week	Number of Lines	Break Batch?	Hours per Wk not Available
1	Formulations	8	5	1		4
2	QC	8	5	1		
3	Filling	14	5	1		4
4	QC	8	5	1		
5	Packing	8	5	1	Yes	
6	Customer Support	8	5	1	Yes	
7	TS	8	5	2	Yes	
8	QA	8	5	1		

Response Time, Lead Time & Inventory Inputs

Task ref	Varieties	RM Min Days Stock	RM Days between Deliveries	Intermed Days Hold Time	Intermed Days Min Sawtooth	Finished Goods Days Hold Time	Finished Goods Days Min Stock
1	17	60	60				
2	17			1			
3	17	30	30				
4	17			4			
5	17	14	14				14
6	17						
7	17						
8	17						

Reagent Kit Factory

The product is in the form of a kit comprising fluids in different bottles, tested, put into a cardboard box and palletized. There is a range of similar products. There are two types of bottle: one is special to each product and one is generic to all.

Product Configuration

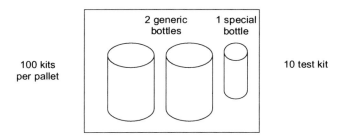

Reagent Kit Flow Diagram

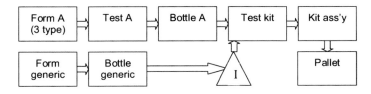

Scenario 28 looks at improving responsiveness.

Scenario 29 looks at a way of saving money by simple product redesign.

#28 Reagent Kit Factory

This is an attempt to minimise Response Time while keeping everything else neutral or better.
The strategy is that used in previous exercises.

Predicted Values   **80,000** items/yr

COST	Material	Other	per item
VOLUME	$80,531	$8,783	$1.116
BATCH		$30,341	$0.379
PRODUCT		$15,000	$0.188
FACILITY		$110,000	$1.375
TOTAL		**$244,656**	**$3.058**

INVENTORY	Material only	ML&O
Raw Material	$34,367	$34,400
WIP	$6,668	$20,300
Finished	$0	$0
All	**$41,035**	**$54,700**

RESPONSE TIME		LEAD TIME
Ship	**58** days	**17** days

CAPACITY	Most Used WorkCenter	
	Formulations **19%**	Utilization

Process Description

Task ref	Activity	Qty per sale	unit	Run waste	Fixed Batch waste	Batch size	Batches per Year	Same Batches per Year as other task?
1	Formulate A	1.00	bottle		800	4,500		
2	Test A		batch					1
3	Bottle compt A	1.00	bottle	5%	50			1
4	Formulate generic	2.00	bottle		50	20,000		
5	Bottle generic	2.00	bottle	1%	10			4
6	Test kit		batch					1
7	Assemble kit	0.10	kit		2			1
8	Ship	0.001	pallet					1

Variable Cost Inputs

Task ref	Activity	Items per Minute	Batch Change over Hours	Manning	Non Value Adding Hours per Hour	Labor Rate per Hour	Employer Costs per Hour	Material Value Added
1	Formulate A		3.0	2	2.0	$10.00	$2.00	$0.30
2	Test A		1.0	1	2.0	$12.00	$3.00	
3	Bottle compt A	60	0.8	3	1.0	$10.00	$2.00	$0.15
4	Formulate generic		10.0	2	2.0	$10.00	$2.00	$0.02
5	Bottle generic	60	0.8	4	2.0	$10.00	$2.00	$0.20
6	Test kit		12.0	1	2.0	$12.00	$3.00	
7	Assemble kit	4	0.5	1	0.5	$10.00	$2.00	$0.70
8	Ship		0.3	1	1.0	$10.00	$2.00	$5.00

Question:
Changing which 2 of the inputs would lead to the differences indicated below?

Differences

Cost Change	Material	Other	per item
VOLUME	-$4,608	$5	-$0.058
BATCH		$3,832	$0.048
PRODUCT		$0	$0.000
FACILITY		$0	$0.000
TOTAL		-$771	-$0.010

Inventory Change	Material only	ML&O
Raw Material	-$4,575	-$4,500
WIP	-$233	$400
Finished	$0	$0
All	-$4,808	-$4,100

Response Time Change		Lead Time Change	
Ship	-8 days	0	days

Capacity Change	Old Most Used W/C		
	Formulations	1%	Utilization Difference

Capacity Inputs

Task ref	Work Center	Spell Hours	Spells per Week	Number of Lines	Break Batch?	Hours per Wk not Available
1	Formulations	8	5	1		4
2	QC	8	5	1		
3	Filling	8	5	1		4
4	Formulations	8	5	1	Yes	
5	Filling	8	5	1		
6	QC	8	5	1	Yes	
7	KA	8	5	1		
8	Despatch	8	5	1		

Response Time, Lead Time & Inventory Inputs

Task ref	Varieties	RM Min Days Stock	RM Days between Deliveries	Intermed Days Hold Time	Intermed Days Min Sawtooth	Finished Goods Days Hold Time	Finished Goods Days Min Stock
1	3	180	360				
2	3						
3	3	60	60				
4	1	60	60				
5	1	30	30	7	0.001		
6	3						
7	3	30	30	7			
8	3			7			

#29 Reagent Kit Factory

This change is the result of a simple product redesign

Predicted Values

80,000 items/yr

COST	Material	Other	per item
VOLUME	$67,350	$5,544	$0.911
BATCH		$23,155	$0.289
PRODUCT		$15,000	$0.188
FACILITY		$110,000	$1.375
TOTAL		$221,049	$2.763

INVENTORY	Material only	ML&O
Raw Material	$36,549	$36,500
WIP	$5,695	$18,700
Finished	$0	$0
All	$42,243	$55,200

RESPONSE TIME		LEAD TIME
Ship	66 days	18 days

CAPACITY	Most Used WorkCenter
	Formulations 16% Utilization

Process Description

Task ref	Activity	Qty per sale	unit	Run waste	Fixed Batch waste	Batch size	Batches per Year	Same Batches per Year as other task?
1	Formulate A	1	bottle		800	4,500		
2	Test A		batch					1
3	Bottle compt A	1	bottle	5%	50			1
4	Formulate generic	2	bottle		50	20,000		
5	Bottle generic	2	bottle	1%	10			4
6	Test kit		batch					1
7	Assemble kit	0.10	kit		2			1
8	Ship	0.001	pallet					1

Variable Cost Inputs

Task ref	Activity	Items per Minute	Batch Change over Hours	Manning	Non Value Adding Hours per Hour	Labor Rate per Hour	Employer Costs per Hour	Material Value Added
1	Formulate A		3.0	2	2.0	$10.00	$2.00	$0.30
2	Test A		1.0	1	2.0	$12.00	$3.00	
3	Bottle compt A	60	0.8	3	1.0	$10.00	$2.00	$0.15
4	Formulate generic		10.0	2	2.0	$10.00	$2.00	$0.02
5	Bottle generic	60	0.8	4	2.0	$10.00	$2.00	$0.20
6	Test kit		12.0	1	2.0	$12.00	$3.00	
7	Assemble kit	4	0.5	1	0.5	$10.00	$2.00	$0.70
8	Ship		0.3	1	1.0	$10.00	$2.00	$5.00

Question:
Changing which 2 of the inputs would lead to the differences indicated below?

Differences

Cost Change	Material	Other	per item
VOLUME	-$17,790	-$3,234	-$0.263
BATCH		-$3,354	-$0.042
PRODUCT		$0	$0.000
FACILITY		$0	$0.000
TOTAL		-$24,378	-$0.305

Inventory Change	Material only	ML&O
Raw Material	-$2,393	-$2,400
WIP	-$1,206	-$1,200
Finished	$0	$0
All	-$3,599	-$3,600

Response Time Change	Lead Time Change
Ship 0 days	0 days

Capacity Change	Old Most Used W/C		
	Formulations	-2%	Utilization Difference

Capacity Inputs

Task ref	Work Center	Spell Hours	Spells per Week	Number of Lines	Break Batch?	Hours per Wk not Available
1	Formulations	8	5	1		4
2	QC	8	5	1		
3	Filling	8	5	1		4
4	Formulations	8	5	1	Yes	
5	Filling	8	5	1		
6	QC	8	5	1	Yes	
7	KA	8	5	1		
8	Despatch	8	5	1		

Response Time, Lead Time & Inventory Inputs

Task ref	Varieties	RM Min Days Stock	RM Days between Deliveries	Intermed Days Hold Time	Intermed Days Min Sawtooth	Finished Goods Days Hold Time	Finished Goods Days Min Stock
1	3	180	360				
2	3						
3	3	60	60				
4	1	60	60				
5	1	30	30	7	0.001		
6	3						
7	3	30	30	7			
8	3			7			

Point of Use Diagnostic Test

This is an individual test for use in (say) a doctor's surgery. This differs from the batch testing often found in specialist laboratories, where the Reagent Test Kit of other examples would be used.

Product Configuration

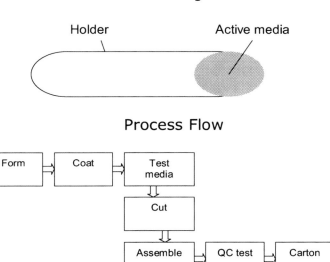

Process Flow

Scenario 30 looks at inventory and time reduction.

Scenario 31 looks at a way of saving money while also improving the other measures. Along the way, the capacity constraint changes.

#30 Point of Use Diagnostic Test

Two separate changes are aimed at reducing inventory and improving responsiveness. One of these increases business risk and would need to be mitigated.

Predicted Values

5,000,000 items/yr

COST	Material	Other	per item
VOLUME	$443,737	$543,209	$0.197
BATCH		$332,046	$0.066
PRODUCT		$45,000	$0.009
FACILITY		$1,595,000	$0.319
TOTAL	**$2,958,992**		**$0.592**

INVENTORY	Material only	ML&O
Raw Material	$53,498	$53,500
WIP	$5,809	$38,700
Finished	$9,254	$61,700
All	**$68,560**	**$153,900**

RESPONSE TIME		LEAD TIME	
Carton	**10** days	**9** days	

CAPACITY	Most Used WorkCenter		
	QC	**87%**	Utilization

Process Description

Task ref	Activity	Qty per sale	unit	Run waste	Fixed Batch waste	Batch size	Batches per Year	Same Batches per Year as other task?
1	Formulate solution	0.01	litre		1	100		
2	Coat media	0.01	m	5%	1			1
3	Test media		batch					1
4	Cut media	1.00	test	10%	20			1
5	Package	1.00	test	1%	2			1
6	QC test		batch					1
7	Carton	0.001	carton					1

Variable Cost Inputs

Task ref	Activity	Items per Minute	Batch Change over Hours	Manning	Non Value Adding Hours per Hour	Labor Rate per Hour	Employer Costs per Hour	Material Value Added
1	Formulate solution		8.0	1	2.0	$20.00	$4.00	$0.40
2	Coat media	0.3	1.0	2	1.0	$20.00	$4.00	$2.00
3	Test media		0.5	1	2.0	$24.00	$6.00	
4	Cut media	100	0.3	1	1.0	$20.00	$4.00	
5	Package	50	0.3	2	1.0	$20.00	$4.00	$0.06
6	QC test		4.0	1	2.0	$24.00	$6.00	
7	Carton	0.2		1	1.0	$20.00	$4.00	$2.00

Question:
Changing which 2 inputs would lead to the differences below?

Answer at www.BridgeoFaith.com

Differences

Cost Change	Material	Other	per item
VOLUME	$0	$0	$0.000
BATCH		$0	$0.000
PRODUCT		$0	$0.000
FACILITY		$0	$0.000
TOTAL		$0	$0.000

Inventory Change	Material only	ML&O
Raw Material	-$41,516	-$41,500
WIP	-$3,565	-$23,800
Finished	$0	$0
All	-$45,081	-$65,300

Response Time Change		Lead Time Change	
Carton	-3 days	-3	days

Capacity Change	Old Most Used W/C	QC	0%	Utilization Difference

Capacity Inputs

Task ref	Work Center	Spell Hours	Spells per Week	Number of Lines	Break Batch?	Hours per Wk not Available
1	Formulations	8	5	2		
2	Coating m/c	8	5	2	Yes	
3	QC	8	5	1		
4	Cutter	8	5	1		
5	Packing	8	5	2		
6	QC	8	5	1		
7	Despatch	8	5	1		

Response Time, Lead Time & Inventory Inputs

Task ref	Varieties	RM Min Days Stock	RM Days between Deliveries	Intermed Days Hold Time	Intermed Days Min Sawtooth	Finished Goods Days Hold Time	Finished Goods Days Min Stock
1	1	90	90	1			
2	1	30	30				
3	1						
4	1						
5	1	60	60				
6	1			5			
7	1	30	30				7

#31 Point of Use Diagnostic Test

This is mostly an attempt to save cost. The result is to improve all measures. The capacity constraint moves from the cutter to QC.

Predicted Values

5,000,000 items/yr

COST	Material	Other	per item
VOLUME	$443,737	$416,556	$0.172
BATCH		$305,196	$0.061
PRODUCT		$45,000	$0.009
FACILITY		$1,595,000	$0.319
TOTAL		**$2,805,489**	**$0.561**

INVENTORY	Material only	ML&O
Raw Material	$95,014	$95,000
WIP	$8,889	$56,200
Finished	$9,254	$58,500
All	**$113,156**	**$209,700**

RESPONSE TIME		LEAD TIME
Carton	**12** days	**11** days

CAPACITY	Most Used WorkCenter
	Cutter **64%** Utilization

Process Description

Task ref	Activity	Qty per sale	unit	Run waste	Fixed Batch waste	Batch size	Batches per Year	Same Batches per Year as other task?
1	Formulate solution	0.01	litre		1	100		
2	Coat media	0.01	m	5%	1			1
3	Test media		batch					1
4	Cut media	1.00	test	10%	20			1
5	Package	1.00	test	1%	2			1
6	QC test		batch					1
7	Carton	0.001	carton					1

Variable Cost Inputs

Task ref	Activity	Items per Minute	Batch Change over Hours	Manning	Non Value Adding Hours per Hour	Labor Rate per Hour	Employer Costs per Hour	Material Value Added
1	Formulate solution		8.0	1	2.0	$20.00	$4.00	$0.40
2	Coat media	0.3	1.0	2	1.0	$20.00	$4.00	$2.00
3	Test media		0.5	1	2.0	$24.00	$6.00	
4	Cut media	100	0.3	1	1.0	$20.00	$4.00	
5	Package	50	0.3	2	1.0	$20.00	$4.00	$0.06
6	QC test		4.0	1	2.0	$24.00	$6.00	
7	Carton	0.2		1	1.0	$20.00	$4.00	$2.00

Question:

Changing which 2 inputs would lead to the differences below?

Answer at www.BridgeoFaith.com

#31

Differences

Cost Change	Material	Other	per item
VOLUME	$0	-$126,653	-$0.025
BATCH		-$26,850	-$0.005
PRODUCT		$0	$0.000
FACILITY		$0	$0.000
TOTAL		-$153,503	-$0.031

Inventory Change	Material only	ML&O
Raw Material	$0	$0
WIP	-$485	-$6,300
Finished	$0	-$3,200
All	-$485	-$9,500

Response Time Change	Lead Time Change
Carton -1 days	-1 days

Capacity Change	Old Most Used W/C	QC	-23%	Utilization Difference

Capacity Inputs

Task ref	Work Center	Spell Hours	Spells per Week	Number of Lines	Break Batch?	Hours per Wk not Available
1	Formulations	8	5	2		
2	Coating m/c	8	5	2	Yes	
3	QC	8	5	1		
4	Cutter	8	5	1		
5	Packing	8	5	2		
6	QC	8	5	1		
7	Despatch	8	5	1		

Response Time, Lead Time & Inventory Inputs

Task ref	Varieties	RM Min Days Stock	RM Days between Deliveries	Intermed Days Hold Time	Intermed Days Min Sawtooth	Finished Goods Days Hold Time	Finished Goods Days Min Stock
1	1	90	90	1			
2	1	30	30				
3	1						
4	1						
5	1	60	60				
6	1			5			
7	1	30	30				7

One Shot Pharmaceutical Product

The product is a plastic disposable filled with a special pharmaceutical liquid. Each one is packed separately and used singly.

Scenario 32 tackles a high material cost by looking at waste. It also makes process adjustments to maximize cost saving without compromising responsiveness.

Scenario 33 looks at a back up proposal to save money if the suggestion of #32 is found to involve too much capital or development expense. Action also has to be taken to maintain responsiveness.

Body Fluid Testing Kit

This product line has 11 variants and is a similar operation to the Reagent Kit of Scenario #28 and #29.

It includes a test tube that is filled partly with a generic solid and partly with a chemical that is unique to each product variant.

Scenario 34 saves money by noticing that batch costs are very high. In order to simultaneously drastically improve responsiveness a review of transport arrangements adds cost but not as much as that saved, leaving a net benefit.

Scenario 35 is similar to Scenario 22. A change is made outside the control of operations that alters everything. In this case the effect is beneficial.

#32 One Shot Pharmaceutical Product

This product has some expensive raw material and a wasteful process. One change saves money, the other brings responsiveness back in line. There is also a significant inventory reduction.

Predicted Values

250,000 items/yr

COST	Material	Other	per item
VOLUME	$1,181,443	$167,122	$5.394
BATCH		$258,938	$1.036
PRODUCT		$0	$0.000
FACILITY		$1,895,000	$7.580
TOTAL		**$3,502,503**	**$14.010**

INVENTORY	Material only	ML&O
Raw Material	$170,355	$170,400
WIP	$21,767	$64,500
Finished	$32,368	$96,000
All	**$224,491**	**$330,900**

RESPONSE TIME		LEAD TIME
Inspect & pack	**41** days	**20** days

CAPACITY	Most Used WorkCenter Utilization
	Packing **65%**

Process Description

Task ref	Activity	Qty per sale	unit	Run waste	Fixed Batch waste	Batch size	Batches per Year	Same Batches per Year as other task?
1	Buy Biological RM	0.02	liter					2
2	Thaw	0.02	liter			200		
3	Purify	0.02	liter	65%				2
4	Ultra filtration	0.02	liter		2			2
5	Test solution		batch	1%				2
6	Fill disposable	1	syringe					2
7	Test disposable		batch	1%				2
8	Inspect & pack	0.2	pack					2

Variable Cost Inputs

Task ref	Activity	Items per Minute	Batch Change over Hours	Manning	Non Value Adding Hours per Hour	Labor Rate per Hour	Employer Costs per Hour	Material Value Added
1	Buy Biological RM							$90.00
2	Thaw		24.0					
3	Purify	0.1	6.0	2	2.0	$20.00	$6.00	
4	Ultra filtration	1	4.0	2	2.0	$20.00	$6.00	$30.00
5	Test solution		8.0	2	2.0	$25.00	$7.00	
6	Fill disposable	40	1.0	2	1.0	$20.00	$6.00	$1.20
7	Test disposable		12.0	4	2.0	$25.00	$7.00	
8	Inspect & pack	12	0.5	3	1.0	$20.00	$6.00	$2.30

Question:
Changing which 2 process inputs would lead to the differences below?

Answer at www.BridgeoFaith.com

Differences

Cost Change	Material	Other	per item
VOLUME	-$698,442	-$151,027	-$3.398
BATCH		-$295,929	-$1.184
PRODUCT		$0	$0.000
FACILITY		$0	$0.000
TOTAL		-$1,145,398	-$4.582

Inventory Change	Material only	ML&O
Raw Material	-$71,424	-$71,400
WIP	-$15,697	-$28,100
Finished	-$19,135	-$31,300
All	-$106,256	-$130,800

Response Time Change	Lead Time Change
Inspect & pack **12** days	**1** days

Capacity Change	Old Most Used W/C	Utilization Difference
	Purification unit	**-9%**

Capacity Inputs

Task ref	Work Center	Spell Hours	Spells per Week	Number of Lines	Break Batch?	Hours per Wk not Available
1						
2		168	1	10		
3	Purification unit	96	1	1		
4	Filtration unit	96	1	1		10
5	QC	8	5	2	Yes	
6	Filling	8	5	1		
7	QC	8	5	2	Yes	
8	Packing	8	5	1		24

Response Time, Lead Time & Inventory Inputs

Task ref	Varieties	RM Min Days Stock	RM Days between Deliveries	Intermed Days Hold Time	Intermed Days Min Sawtooth	Finished Goods Days Hold Time	Finished Goods Days Min Stock
1	1	30	14				
2	1						
3	1						
4	1	90	90				
5	2			2			
6	2	30	30				
7	2						
8	2	30	30			10	

#33 One Shot Pharmaceutical Product

The improvement of the previous example is found not to be feasible. Here is an attempt to save money by another method while maintaining responsiveness.

Predicted Values

250,000 items/yr

COST	Material	Other	per item
VOLUME	$1,878,435	$318,024	$8.786
BATCH		$369,911	$1.480
PRODUCT		$0	$0.000
FACILITY		$1,895,000	$7.580
TOTAL		**$4,461,370**	**$17.845**

INVENTORY	Material only	ML&O
Raw Material	$241,243	$241,200
WIP	$41,063	$97,500
Finished	$15,439	$36,700
All	**$297,746**	**$375,400**

RESPONSE TIME		LEAD TIME	
Inspect & pack	**28** days	**13** days	

CAPACITY	Most Used WorkCenter Utilization
	Purification unit **80%**

Process Description

Task ref	Activity	Qty per sale	unit	Run waste	Fixed Batch waste	Batch size	Batches per Year	Same Batches per Year as other task?
1	Buy Biological RM	0.02	liter					2
2	Thaw	0.02	liter			200		
3	Purify	0.02	liter	65%				2
4	Ultra filtration	0.02	liter		2			2
5	Test solution		batch	1%				2
6	Fill disposable	1	syringe					2
7	Test disposable		batch	1%				2
8	Inspect & pack	0.2	pack					2

Variable Cost Inputs

Task ref	Activity	Items per Minute	Batch Change over Hours	Manning	Non Value Adding Hours per Hour	Labor Rate per Hour	Employer Costs per Hour	Material Value Added
1	Buy Biological RM							$90.00
2	Thaw		24.0					
3	Purify	0.1	6.0	2	2.0	$20.00	$6.00	
4	Ultra filtration	1	4.0	2	2.0	$20.00	$6.00	$30.00
5	Test solution		8.0	2	2.0	$25.00	$7.00	
6	Fill disposable	40	1.0	2	1.0	$20.00	$6.00	$1.20
7	Test disposable		12.0	4	2.0	$25.00	$7.00	
8	Inspect & pack	12	0.5	3	1.0	$20.00	$6.00	$2.30

Question:
Changing which 2 inputs would lead to the differences below?

Differences

Cost Change	Material	Other	per item
VOLUME	-$1,450	-$126	-$0.006
BATCH		-$184,956	-$0.740
PRODUCT		$0	$0.000
FACILITY		$0	$0.000
TOTAL		-$186,532	-$0.746

Inventory Change	Material only	ML&O
Raw Material	-$536	-$600
WIP	$3,600	$4,900
Finished	-$36,065	-$90,600
All	-$33,001	-$86,300

Response Time Change	Lead Time Change
Inspect & pack **-1** days	**-6** days

Capacity Change	Old Most Used W/C Utilization Difference
	Purification unit **6%**

Capacity Inputs

Task ref	Work Center	Spell Hours	Spells per Week	Number of Lines	Break Batch?	Hours per Wk not Available
1						
2		168	1	10		
3	Purification unit	96	1	1		
4	Filtration unit	96	1	1		10
5	QC	8	5	2	Yes	
6	Filling	8	5	1		
7	QC	8	5	2	Yes	
8	Packing	8	5	1		24

Response Time, Lead Time & Inventory Inputs

Task ref	Varieties	RM Min Days Stock	RM Days between Deliveries	Intermed Days Hold Time	Intermed Days Min Sawtooth	Finished Goods Days Hold Time	Finished Goods Days Min Stock
1	1	30	14				
2	1						
3	1						
4	1	90	90				
5	2			2			
6	2	30	30				
7	2						
8	2	30	30			10	

#34 Body Fluid Testing Kit

The excessively high batch related costs are the target for cost reduction here. However, another change that costs extra money is needed in order to also improve responsiveness.

Predicted Values

860,000 items/yr

COST	Material	Other	per item
VOLUME	$130,564	$47,857	$0.207
BATCH		$362,015	$0.421
PRODUCT		$112,000	$0.130
FACILITY		$608,000	$0.707
TOTAL	**$1,260,436**		**$1.466**

INVENTORY	Material only	ML&O
Raw Material	$36,118	$36,100
WIP	$2,136	$20,600
Finished	$2,511	$24,200
All	**$40,765**	**$80,900**

RESPONSE TIME		LEAD TIME	
Ship	**17** days	**1** days	

CAPACITY	Most Used WorkCenter		
	Truck	**77%**	Utilization

Process Description

Task ref	Activity	Qty per sale	unit	Run waste	Fixed Batch waste	Batch size	Batches per Year	Same Batches per Year as other task?
1	Pretreat RM	0.0008	liter	15%	1	20		
2	Make generic	0.0020	kg	35%	5	100		
3	Formulate reagent A	0.80	ml		150			7
4	Fill test tube	1.00	tube		250			7
5	Test		batch					7
6	Calibrate		batch					7
7	Pack	0.02	pack				572	
8	Ship	0.00015	truck			1.0		

Variable Cost Inputs

Task ref	Activity	Items per Minute	Batch Change over Hours	Manning	Non Value Adding Hours per Hour	Labor Rate per Hour	Employer Costs per Hour	Material Value Added
1	Pretreat RM		24.0	1	2.0	$22.00	$6.00	$84.07
2	Make generic	1.2	3.0	1	2.0	$22.00	$6.00	$9.00
3	Formulate reagent A		3.0	1	2.0	$22.00	$6.00	
4	Fill test tube	80	0.8	3	1.0	$20.00	$6.00	$0.02
5	Test		3.0	1	2.0	$25.00	$7.00	
6	Calibrate		2.0	1	2.0	$25.00	$7.00	
7	Pack	3	0.2	4	0.5	$20.00	$5.00	$0.80
8	Ship		24.0	1		$10.00		

34

Question:
Changing which 2 inputs would lead to the differences below?

Differences

Cost Change	Material	Other	per item
VOLUME	-$1,430	-$2,324	-$0.004
BATCH		-$218,289	-$0.254
PRODUCT		$0	$0.000
FACILITY		$0	$0.000
TOTAL		-$222,043	-$0.258

Inventory Change	Material only	ML&O
Raw Material	-$353	-$400
WIP	$16	-$3,200
Finished	$1,242	$9,900
All	$905	$6,300

Response Time Change		Lead Time Change	
Ship	**-16** days	0	days

Capacity Change	Old Most Used W/C		
	Formulations	**11%**	Utilization Difference

Capacity Inputs

Task ref	Work Center	Spell Hours	Spells per Week	Number of Lines	Break Batch?	Hours per Wk not Available
1	Pretreat	8	5	1	Yes	2
2	Formulations	8	5	2		4
3	Formulations	8	5	2		
4	Filling	8	5	1		4
5	QC	8	5	2		
6	Calibration	8	5	1		
7	Packing	8	5	1		
8	Truck	168	1	1		

Response Time, Lead Time & Inventory Inputs

Task ref	Varieties	RM Min Days Stock	RM Days between Deliveries	Intermed Days Hold Time	Intermed Days Min Sawtooth	Finished Goods Days Hold Time	Finished Goods Days Min Stock
1	11	90	90				
2	1	30	30	1			
3	11						
4	11	60	60				
5	11			1			
6	11						
7	11	30	14				0
8	11						

#35 Body Fluid Testing Kit

One process input has changed, but not because of a change in process!

Predicted Values

860,000 items/yr

COST	Material	Other	per item
VOLUME	$135,880	$49,758	$0.216
BATCH		$534,986	$0.622
PRODUCT		$101,818	$0.118
FACILITY		$608,000	$0.707
TOTAL		**$1,430,442**	**$1.663**

INVENTORY	Material only	ML&O
Raw Material	$37,940	$37,900
WIP	$11,305	$119,000
Finished	$1,307	$13,800
All	**$50,552**	**$170,700**

RESPONSE TIME		LEAD TIME
Ship	**29** days	**1** days

CAPACITY	Most Used WorkCenter	
	Formulations	**62%** Utilization

Process Description

Task ref	Activity	Qty per sale	unit	Run waste	Fixed Batch waste	Batch size	Batches per Year	Same Batches per Yr as other task?
1	Pretreat RM	0.0008	liter	15%	1	20		
2	Make generic	0.0020	kg	35%	5	100		
3	Formulate reagent A	0.80	ml		150			7
4	Fill test tube	1.00	tube		250			7
5	Test		batch					7
6	Calibrate		batch					7
7	Pack	0.02	pack				520	
8	Ship	0.00015	truck			1		

Variable Cost Inputs

Task ref	Activity	Items per Minute	Batch Change over Hours	Manning	Non Value Adding Hours per Hour	Labor Rate per Hour	Employer Costs per Hour	Material Value Added
1	Pretreat RM		24.0	1	2.0	$22.00	$6.00	$88.84
2	Make generic	1.2	3.0	1	2.0	$22.00	$6.00	$9.00
3	Formulate reagent A		3.0	1	2.0	$22.00	$6.00	
4	Fill test tube	80	0.8	3	1.0	$20.00	$6.00	$0.02
5	Test		3.0	1	2.0	$25.00	$7.00	
6	Calibrate		2.0	1	2.0	$25.00	$7.00	
7	Pack	3	0.2	4	0.5	$20.00	$5.00	$0.80
8	Ship		24.0	1		$10.00		

35

Question:
What other change has caused both this change and the differences seen below?

Answer at www.BridgeoFaith.com

Differences

Cost Change	Material	Other	per item
VOLUME	$3,886	-$423	$0.004
BATCH		-$45,318	-$0.053
PRODUCT		-$10,182	-$0.012
FACILITY		$0	$0.000
TOTAL		-$52,037	-$0.061

Inventory Change	Material only	ML&O
Raw Material	$1,469	$1,400
WIP	-$263	-$10,900
Finished	$37	-$500
All	$1,244	-$10,000

Response Time Change		Lead Time Change	
Ship	-3 days	0	days

Capacity Change	Old Most Used W/C		
	Formulations	-5%	Utilization Difference

Capacity Inputs

Task ref	Work Center	Spell Hours	Spells per Week	Number of Lines	Break Batch?	Hours per Wk not Available
1	Pretreat	8	5	1	Yes	2
2	Formulations	8	5	2		4
3	Formulations	8	5	2		
4	Filling	8	5	1		4
5	QC	8	5	2		
6	Calibration	8	5	1		
7	Packing	8	5	1		
8	Truck	168	1	1		

Response Time, Lead Time & Inventory Inputs

Task ref	Varieties	RM Min Days Stock	RM Days between Deliveries	Intermed Days Hold Time	Intermed Days Min Sawtooth	Finished Goods Days Hold Time	Finished Goods Days Min Stock
1	11	90	90		1		
2	1	30	30	1			
3	11						
4	11	60	60				
5	11			1			
6	11						
7	11	30	14				0.001
8	11						

8. Closer Look at the Body Fluid Testing Kit

Let's examine the Body Fluid Testing Kit operation of Scenarios 34 & 35 in more depth.

In the scenario summary tables you see the totals for all processes. We will now look in greater depth by looking at cost, inventory, time and capacity elements by activity and work center.

Cost first:

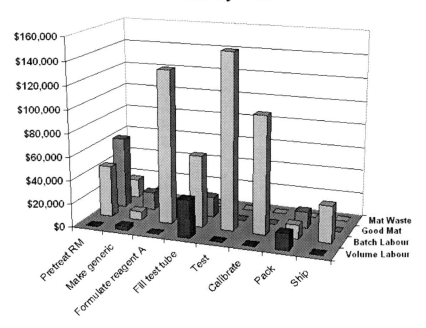

Cost by Process

Material, waste and labor cost is charted for each process as a Manhattan Diagram.

Material waste is separated from the "good" material that is actually contained in the product that the customer receives. The largest material cost is for the pretreated raw material at about $60,000 per year. However, the most striking observation is that there are high batch related labor costs across many processes. In fact, the highest bar relates to the testing step.

If the testing effort were reduced by 20%, the annual saving would be about $30,000 per year.

However, another way of saving money is to make fewer batches, i.e. make larger batches. As you saw, most of these processes are linked together. So, if you increased batch size throughout, you save batch related expense on all of them. A 20% increase in batch size would thus save $100,000.

Unfortunately, increasing batch size has a negative effect on response time: larger batch size means a longer time between batches. Time between batches is one of the factors that make up response time. To compensate for this, extra transport was suggested in Scenario 34 that added cost. Not good for the transport manager's budget, but good for the business overall.

Of course, there may be a negative impact on other measures which should be looked at.

What about the inventory picture? The Manhattan Diagram for material inventory value looks like this:

Material Value of Inventory

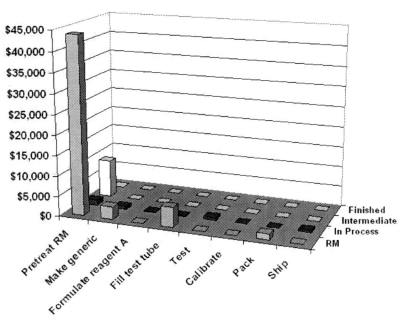

Most of the value is tied up as raw material. This is not affected by changes in batch size downstream.

However, there is another effect for a different reason. There was a product change in Scenario 35: one product was phased out and the sales replaced by an equal amount of one of the other products. The raw material purchase price for the substituted material is more. The raw material value of 'x' days of stock thus increases in proportion. This small change is seen in the summary for scenario 35.

There are also some subtle effects on WIP: intermediate stock drops because there are fewer variants held in this form, while In Process inventory increases to correspond to more material associated with a larger batch.

What about time? This chart shows the constituents of Lead Time.

Lead Time Build Up

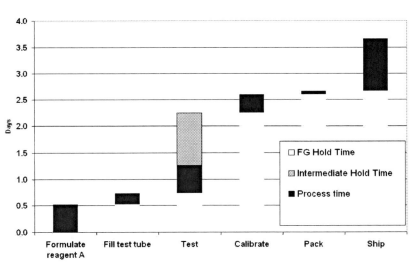

If you wanted to reduce lead time you might start by reducing the hold time after test. This would also reduce response time. However, another way to reduce response time is by doing things more frequently. In this case, shipping 20% more often would reduce response time by 5 days. As noted for scenario 34, there is an added cost for the extra shipments.

All of these changes must be done while maintaining sufficient spare capacity. In Scenario 34 the utilization of the truck increased to 77%, but this is acceptable.

Meanwhile in the factory itself the capacity picture by work center looks like this:

Capacity Utilisation

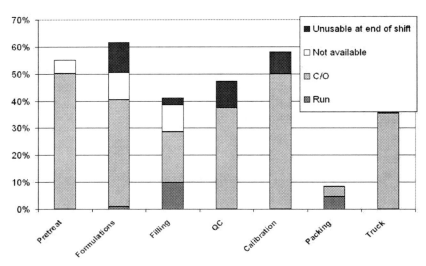

The formulations area is used most, but only by a few percent. Any attempt to improve this, by eliminating the time the work center is not available (say), moves the capacity constraint first to the calibration area and then to the pre-treat area. In the end, you would probably add capacity by adding extra shifts.

Summary

The only change that is not a compromise is one where all business measures get better, or at least none get worse.

This is almost true for these two scenarios.

Eliminating one product variant, as in Scenario 35, saves money, time, and capacity. The inventory picture is less clear: material inventory rises slightly, although the finance people will love the apparent drop in the fully-burdened value.

Scenario 34 looks more compelling. Cost and responsiveness improve dramatically with a capacity penalty that is bearable and an inventory change largely from enlarged finished goods stock.

9. FURTHER APPLICATION

The Bridge Of Faith for Operations approach makes you better understand your operation viewed from the whole.

You can use it first to convince yourself that a change is worthwhile. Armed with the logic and the numbers, you can explain it convincingly to everybody else involved: your colleagues, the boss, your subordinates or anybody else in the organization, including other departments such as marketing or R&D.

As a result you will be able to save time, money, inventory and capacity, while knowing where to deploy your team.

We also hope that we have managed to dispel the belief that you need to change everything to get everything to change. There are some simple things that you can do that change everything. You need to find the specific effective action on which you must focus your attention.

You can turn this approach into an Operations Model by using the spreadsheet templates available through the **www.BridgeoFaith.com** web site. These enable you to test a wide range of "what if?" scenarios by instantly recalculating everything for you.

You can test ideas within your operation.

You can also check ideas that are instigated in other parts of the business.

Some examples:

1. Sales Volume and Product Mix

The latest sales forecast shows that sales will increase by 10% (say), but this is not uniform across the product range. Some products have increases larger than this and some will decline. You can answer questions like these:

Do we still have capacity?

Will we have to change our shift pattern?

What will be the effect on cost and inventory?

2. Addition of New Product to Portfolio

Marketing wish to add a new product to the portfolio. This will also affect the sales of other products. Answer these:

Will it affect capacity?

How will unit cost change?

What do you have to do to maintain the responsiveness that you have now?

3. New Product Concept

This is possibly the highest value use of the Bridge of Faith approach. It is much easier to improve an operation before you ever create one. You can predict how it will look by using your best guesses about processes, costs, timings. Then you will be able to steer the R&D people in the best direction and quantify these and other issues:

What design alternatives would make the operation more responsive?

What design features are going to make it difficult to drive cost below a certain point?

Which parts should be common to all products?

How much strategic inventory is going to be inherent in using scarce raw materials?

How could the quality assurance process be streamlined to minimize lead time?

4. Revision of Distribution System

How much stock is going to be necessary to provide the responsiveness demanded by customers?

Are transport costs traded off against manufacturing costs?

How much will total inventory change?

5. Rationalization of Multiple Sites

Suppose you make similar products at a range of sites. Faced with rationalization proposals, you will be able to answer these questions:

What will be the true difference in manufacturing cost by moving from one to another?

What are the real strengths of each production line in terms of responsiveness, inventory and capacity?

Which facilities are more adaptable to changes in product mix?

10. WHAT NEXT?

Getting Answers

Answers and fuller explanations for each scenario in this book can be found at **www.BridgeoFaith.com.**

Operations Templates

Working through the scenarios in this book forces you to understand the issues.

Now that you do, you may wish to avoid all the manual calculations and guesswork and quickly get the answers you want. The scenarios of this book were created using a spreadsheet based Operations Template that takes out all the hard work.

Get hold of them by contacting us at **www.BridgeoFaith.com**

Further Help

Further books, CD's and online resources in the Bridge Of Faith series will expand on these topics.

You will also find a link for email help at the web site **www.BridgeoFaith.com**

Meanwhile, we wish you well in your endeavors to bring your people along with your operations improvement plans.

11. INDEX OF OPERATIONAL ISSUES

This list gives the Scenario reference number that covers particular issues:

References

Cooper R, Kaplan RS (1991) The Design of Cost Management Systems. Prentice Hall, Upper Saddle River, USA

La Trobe-Bateman J, Wild DG (2003) Design for manufacturing: use of a spreadsheet model of manufacturability to optimize product design and development. Springer Verlag

Bridge of Faith for Operations series Submission Form

Please share *your* "Bridge of Faith" stories with us at
www.BridgeoFaith.com or stories@BridgeoFaith.com

Using our dear friend and colleague Laura Benjamin's C.A.R.L.A
Concept™ below to best communicate your experience, how has
the *Bridge of Faith* for Operations series shown you how to
improve your business?

C.ircumstances faced:

A.ctions taken:

R.esults achieved:

L.essons learned:

A.lternative approach:

___ Yes, you can share my story

___ Yes, you can use my name

Signed: _____

Also, to find out more about Laura Benjamin's exciting new book C.A.R.L.A.
Concept™ please go to www.CarlaConcept.com

*"If you don't know where you're going,
any road will take you there."*   George Harrison

CPSIA information can be obtained at www.ICGtesting.com
Printed in the USA
BVOW012104191212

308710BV00002B/2/A